Throne Room *of my* Heart

by Sharon Corbett

Riverain Publishing

ISBN: 978-0-9932954-0-9

Throne Room of my Heart

"Romantic, inspiring out of this world! You would be forgiven for thinking that this book is the stuff that 'dreams are made of' but you would be wrong. The enchantment of this book lies in the fact that it is based on a true story.

For those of you who have been disillusioned by the dryness of religion, this book will give you renewed hope and the desire to 'dream again your own dreams' and believe that you too can enter into the 'Throne Room of Your Heart."

Sheila Hendley

Dedication

Tramaine and Juvonne with all my love.
To a beautiful woman who I have adopted as my Mom,
you have been my inspiration.

Ephesians 3:20

"God can do anything, you know - far more than you
could ever imagine or guess or request in your wildest
dreams! He does it not by pushing us around but by
working within us, his Spirit deeply
and gently within us." MSG

Throne Room of my Heart

by Sharon Corbett

Chapter 1
Mama

A loud noise rang in my ears as I turned under my cool sheets. Slowly opening my eyes, I peered across the room. All the beds were empty, only I was left asleep. The familiar sound of Mama's voice came from the kitchen. I took a deep breath inhaling the warm smell of fresh bread which made my tummy rumble. I swung my little legs off the bed and wiggled my toes into the woven mat. My jelly shoes weren't at the edge of the mat where I had left them last night. Sleepily venturing barefoot across the hall in the direction of Mama's voice, I could hear the hustle and bustle of pots and pans and the sound of excited chatter.

I peered around the kitchen door, and watched quietly as Mama and her helpers were busy at work. Maisie was by the sink peeling vegetables, the morning sun from the window shining on her curly black hair. She was a short, round woman and when she smiled, which she often did, her teeth were as white as milk and when she spoke, her voice was soft and childlike. I can't ever remember seeing her cross or unhappy. Then there was Grammy, she was very tall, her skin was a light tan colour with freckles, which got darker when she was in the sun. I don't really know what her hair was like or what colour it was, because she always had it tied with a floral headscarf. Grammy was always humming while she worked, which sometimes annoyed Mama, but she was kind and gentle with sparkly eyes which made you forgive her quickly. I walked over to Mama, sucking my two middle fingers, and held onto her skirt longing to taste the warm bread that was cooling.

"Good morning sleepyhead," her voice tender and melodious as she bent down and kissed my cheek, her hands still in the dough she was kneading. I snuggled closer to her legs and rested my head against her, making my neatly twisted hair cover my eyes. Mama was always calm. I can't ever remember being scolded or pushed away, only kisses and lots of hugs from her soft arms. She was beautiful, with small even lips, light brown skin and long dark hair which she kept in a plaited bun. Although I wasn't the only child in the house, she kept me close to her.

"Your mother is coming today so you better go find Myrtle," she said while walking to the sink and washing her hands. "She needs to get you dressed and comb your hair," she added ruffling her hands through my twists. I held tightly onto her skirt as she walked across the kitchen. Her words confused me. I didn't understand what she was saying. *My mother, coming, what did Mama mean?* She reached into the cookie jar and handed me a biscuit. I released my fingers from my mouth and took the biscuit, but still clung onto her skirt. Something wasn't right, but I didn't know what it was.

"Beth, be a good girl for Mama and go get dressed. Whatever is wrong with you?" She picked me up as she went into the corridor and shouted for Myrtle. I hugged her tightly as if my life depended on it, my little heart pounding. Myrtle came and Mama tried to hand me over, but I held even tighter to her neck and refused to let go.

"No Mama," I cried, kicking my legs out as Myrtle held my waist tightly. I let out a loud scream, Myrtle suddenly let go.

"I never hurt her! She's just playing me up because you're here. Behave yourself, Beth," Myrtle scowled.

"Never mind Myrtle, go to the kitchen and help the others while I get her ready. God only knows what's wrong with this child this morning!" Myrtle frowned and narrowed her eyes at me, but did as she was told. Mama patted my back, cradling me in her arms as she carried me to the bedroom.

"Beth, your Mother is coming today and I have lots to do before she arrives. You are going to have to go outside and play with the others when you are dressed. I really don't know why Myrtle didn't wake you up earlier! I will have to have words with her."

"But Mama," I said slowly, "I don't want a new mother," I whined kicking my legs in frustration.

"Oh sweetheart, she's not a new mother, she is your Mother and she wants you to live with her." She put her arms around me and held me close.

"My mother? But you're my Mother." I couldn't understand it. I had lived with Mama my whole life, I had not known any other. "I don't want to live with her, I want to stay with you!" Tears of defiance streamed down my face.

"Oh dear, I should have told you sooner, I'm your Grandmother and your Mother wants you and your sisters to live with her." Mama drew me closer, her face filled with pain. "There was never a right time to tell you, I have loved you as my own, hush now child, hush." Regret filled her voice as she rocked my little body back and forth attempting to soothe me.

I was silent now, fiddling with my hands, trying to make sense of it all. Mama's eyes were red with tears - I had made her cry. I had never seen her cry before. I leaned on her chest as she stroked my hair. I didn't mean to make her sad.

"Sorry Mama," I snuggled into her.

"No child, it's not your fault, this is just how things go sometimes. Dry your eyes, Baby."

I slipped off the bed, took my towel and dried my eyes. Climbing onto Mama's lap, I then took the towel and wiped her eyes. She smiled reaching behind her for my dress. I raised my arms as my cool cotton dress slid onto me.

"Go on my darling, go and play now," Mama ushered me off her lap, and I obediently walked towards the veranda looking out thoughtfully. Rover was lying in the shade away from the hot sun, lazily stretched out. As if sensing my unhappiness, he got up, slowly walked over and reassuringly nuzzled into me.

"Rover we are going to be leaving here soon," I looked into his puppy dog eyes, "but don't worry I'm going to look after you." I assured him.

I rested my head into his soft warm fur and carried on looking out at the yard.

Our front yard was made up of a large playing area with swings and toys. I looked over to the big ball pitch, with its green grass, tall trees and berry hedges, where the cricket and baseball tournaments were played every year. Hundreds of spectators would come from all over the island with their food baskets, to watch as the men competed. The children always looked forward to these events, because we had lots of treats like, coconut drops, cassava bread, roti, snowball, peanut fudge, to name a few. Mama let us take turns to rotate the handle on the ice cream churn - it made the creamiest ice cream you have ever tasted! Licking my lips I smiled at the thought and hoped I wouldn't be taken too far away from all the things I loved most.

Judith's laughter interrupted my thoughts. She had caught Becca and they fell on the grass laughing. *How could they laugh? How could they be so happy?* I sighed, as more tears rolled from my eyes onto Rover's fur. *Didn't they realise someone was coming to take us away from our Mama?* I watched the other children as they chased each other playing tag. *Maybe they knew we weren't going far, that's why they were all so happy,* I thought to myself.

I closed my eyes to block out the early morning sun and wondered how far away this stranger they called my mother lived. Curling up closer to Rover, I thought about Uncle Tom and all the beautiful houses he had built. *Maybe he would build us a house up by the plantation, or better still, down the road by Mrs Whiteman.* Her house was close to the river where all the women did the washing, but most of all, it wouldn't be too far away from Mama.

As I hugged Rover, stroking his short creamy fur, an awful thought came to me. I sat up quickly, startling Rover - he whined in protest. *What if she doesn't like dogs, like Millie who worked at the bakery?* Millie was so scared of dogs that someone always had to meet her down by the lane and walk her across the yard when she came to visit Mama. *What if I have to leave my dog, my Rover behind?* I shook my head - it didn't bear thinking about.

Myrtle came out of the house and stood behind me.

"Girl, you always have that finger in your mouth," she poked my shoulders as she went past and sat on the veranda steps. "What's wrong with you now? Why you crying?" I looked down, hiding my face. She pushed a flannel into my hands, "You better get up and dry those tears. Your mother will be here soon."

I rolled my eyes and turned away from her. Myrtle was always telling me what to do and bossing me around. It was just because she was the eldest and Mama put her in charge of us. With nine children living with Mama, Myrtle had her hands full, which wasn't her idea of fun. I knew better than not to listen to her though, so I got up and walked back into the house, Rover at my heels.

Everyone was excited about my mother's arrival. I watched from behind Mama as the car pulled up into the yard. The car door opened and a small child was handed to my aunt. *So she had a child, then why did she want to take us away!* I held tightly onto Mama's skirt and squeezed my eyes shut, afraid of what I might see. Maybe she had horns, big teeth, red eyes and hair growing from her chin, just like the stepmother in the story Myrtle read to us last night. The woman stepped out of the car and I heard everyone greeting her. Her voice didn't sound like a monster so I opened my eyes and peered around Mama's skirt to take a better look. She was a little darker than Mama, around the same height. I saw no hair on her chin or horns on her head. She bent down and looked around Mama's skirt to where I was hiding. I snuggled closer into Mama's legs almost knocking her over. Mama caught her footing and grabbed my arm to stop me landing on the ground.

"Beth! Careful!" She stood me up in front of the woman who smiled gently and took my hands in hers. I looked down at them, warm and soft, nothing like I had expected. *No*, I tried to pull my hands away, *she is not my mother*. I looked up at Mama, but she didn't intervene.

"My how you've grown!" she came closer and hugged me. I stood as stiff as a board. I looked into her eyes which appeared to twinkle in the sun. They were not as red as I had imagined, and when she smiled, her teeth were as white as Maisie's. She had black straight hair which fell past her shoulders, her face smooth and beautiful like Mama's. I relaxed a little as she let go of my hand, and I grabbed back onto Mama's skirt. I watched as she put her arm around Mama's shoulder talking and laughing, as they both walked into the shade of the house.

During the following weeks, I noticed that the woman they called my mother, paid special attention to me and three of the other children in the house. It was only then that I realised I only had four sisters. Pamela, who arrived with my mother, was two years old. She seemed quite small for her age and had lots of thick, black curly hair which made her cry every time it was combed. She never spoke and couldn't walk or hold things in her hands like I could, but she smiled when I talked to her or pulled funny faces. My mother kept her by her side and never allowed Myrtle to wash, change or feed her. Then there was Dana who was four, Judith who was six and Becca who was five years old like me. At the time I thought nothing of it and no one thought to tell us that we were twins. Myrtle didn't bathe us, put us to bed, or read us stories anymore - my mother did. I struggled to accept the interference by this woman in my life. Every time I went to Mama she would find a reason to draw me away. Mama's eyes didn't sparkle anymore. Whenever I ignored my mother's instructions, she would say, "Go on Beth, do as your mother says," and because I didn't want to upset her, I obeyed. There were many nights I would wake up screaming for Mama. Some nights Mama came to console me and take me to her room, so as not to wake the others. She would cuddle me and rock me back to sleep. On other nights my mother would come and put her arms around me.

"Shhh, it's ok. Mummy is here now," but I wouldn't be consoled and Mama would have to come.

"You go and get some rest Ruth. I'll see to her. You have the little one to see to." My mother would reluctantly leave the room, then Mama would take me into her bed and I would fall asleep.

My mother wasn't at all happy about what was now becoming my nightly routine. One morning I woke up to raised voices.

"How am I supposed to get her more independent if you don't let me handle her? When she gets to England I won't have time to baby her like you do. I have a sick child that needs my undivided attention. Beth isn't sick anymore. The doctor told me her heart and lungs are doing just fine."

"So if Pamela takes up so much of your time, why are you taking the children to England, where you have no support?"

"They are my children and I want them with me." My mother's voice broke as she began to cry. "I'm grateful Mama, for everything but it's time now."

I peered through the gap in the door. My mother was leaning on the kitchen sink. Mama walked over to where she was standing and put her arms around her.

"Ruth, leave the children until Pamela is older and

then take them," she said, patting her on the back like she did to me when I was upset.

"No Mama I need them with me. They don't even know me!" She pulled away and sat on a chair by the table.

"Okay, I understand that. Then take two of them and when things settle down send for the other two." Mama sat down and handed her daughter a cloth to dry her eyes. Both women sat in silence for a while. My mother was the first to speak.

"Okay, I'll take Judith and Beth." She rose to her feet as my heart sank. I wanted to scream "Nooo!" but instead I slid to the floor in the corner and tried my hardest to muffle the sound that threatened to erupt from my mouth. I waited until my mother left the kitchen, and then ran into Mama's arms tears streaming down my face. Mama cried too rocking me as she always did.

"How many times have I told you not to listen in on adult conversation, Beth?" She turned my face towards hers, her eyes swollen from crying. I didn't speak, sadness had taken my voice. "Always remember that I love you my precious. God will take care of you and your sisters. If you listen carefully, you will hear Him and you will know He is there. Do as your mother says and everything will be ok." She hugged me tight and kissed the top of my head. "Now dry those tears and be a brave girl for Mama. Go and get yourself dressed and show your mother what a big girl you are." Her voice broke with every word. She started to hum a familiar song 'God will take care of you[1] which made me stand up tall. I was going to be brave.

Months passed quickly and before I knew it, the fateful day had arrived for me to travel to England with my mother, Judith and Pamela. I refused to cry anymore, I had no choice, the decision had been made, and I had resolved that I was going to England. The sun was shining like it usually did every morning, except for the rainy season. It was spring and all the flowers in the garden looked especially beautiful. My Uncle arrived with the van and packed the suitcases and bags into the trunk. Mama hugged and kissed me. I tried not to cry as she reminded me to be brave. She kissed Pamela, and hugged and kissed Judith as she fought back the tears. Maisie and Grammy cried as they hugged us and said their goodbyes. There were so many people waving as we climbed into the van. I couldn't see Myrtle - I hadn't said goodbye to her. *And, where's my precious Rover?* I had to leave him behind. Mama told me that I couldn't take him, because he wasn't allowed on the aeroplane so she would look after him. My heart skipped a beat as the van engine revved into gear. I kept repeating Mama's words, *I am a brave girl, I am a brave girl,* as we drove down the lane, onto the main road, and out of sight of everything I knew and loved. It was then that I heard a whisper,

I will take care of you.

It sounded just like Mama. I slipped my hand into Judith's arm and snuggled close to her.

---

[1] 'God will take care of you' Lyrics by Civilla D Martin (1904)

16

The airport was noisy with planes coming and going. I had never been to an airport before and I wasn't sure that I liked it. My mother didn't talk to us except to tell us to sit out of the sun and then she had a short conversation with my Uncle. We didn't have to wait long before our flight came in. Uncle Tom pointed to the aeroplane with B.O.A.C written in big letters on its side.

"The house must be very far away," I said to Judith looking up at the huge plane.

"Yes silly, it's in England," she said pushing me with her shoulders.

"Yes my little one, it's very far away," my Uncle said softly as he picked me up and sat me on his lap. "We will miss you both." His voice was sad as he spoke.

He put his arms around us hugging us tight, and nothing more was said. He stayed until it was time to board and looked very smart in his police uniform, as he waved goodbye to us at the boarding gate. My mother carried Pamela and told Judith and I to hold hands and follow her. Mama's voice echoed in my head and I held tightly onto Judith as we climbed the steps of the aeroplane.

We were shown to our seats by a smartly dressed steward, who also helped my mother pack our bags in the overhead compartment. It was cool inside the plane, with rows and rows of seats and little windows that didn't open. Judith sat by the window and I sat in the middle seat next to my mother. I wanted to sit by the window so that I could see, so I pushed closer to Judith, and we both peered out. We felt very tall so far above the ground. It wasn't long before we were buckled up and the plane took off. All the houses and trees below looked so tiny, as the plane soared into the sky. Judith and I giggled, we were flying. But soon the sensation of the plane made my tummy feel woozy and it wasn't long before my mother was to find out that I was travel sick. I wondered if she wished she had left me with Mama after all.

Chapter 2
Torn

My stomach churned again as I put my head back into the paper bag the stewardess had handed me. Closing my eyes in a sleepy haze, I imagined being back with Mama, her delicate hands stroking my head and rocking me back and forth. If she were here, I wouldn't be sitting with the stewards while my mother was back there with my sisters.

"Hi little one, aren't you a big girl sitting up front here with me. How old are you, then?" I looked up at the stewardess, a kind face with ginger hair pulled tightly back in a bun. One of her wavy curls had escaped into her face, and she tucked it behind her ears as she smiled down at me.

Instinctively I showed her the palm of my hand with my fingers all spread out and grinned.

"I'm five," I said proudly.

"Wow! You are a big girl then. And very brave, this is a rough plane ride for you, isn't it?" I nodded as I pulled my cardigan tighter around me, the air seemed to get colder and my skin began to feel prickly.

"Awh you're cold, aren't you? We'll be landing in England soon - it will be much colder than where you've come from. I'll go get you a blanket." I shivered again, *why was it so cold?* The stewardess returned with a dark, grey, woolly blanket and wrapped it around my legs.

"Thank you," I said through chattering teeth. I pulled it up around my shoulders. Judith appeared over the headrest of my seat.

"Are you ok, Beth?"

"It's freezing, have you got a blanket too?"

"Nope, it's so cold I can't feel my toes in these sandals." Judith curled up next to me under my blanket, our body heat warming us up. A loud voice boomed from the tannoy.

"Please return to your seats, and secure your seatbelts, we are getting ready to land. Welcome to England."

"Come on then, buckle up your seat belt. Oh hello, shall I get you a blanket too?" Judith nodded and then frowned as we reluctantly pulled away from each other into our own seats. The stewardess placed the blanket around Judith. "What pretty dresses you girls are wearing." We beamed back at her. I looked down at my tulle dress that Mama had made for me. I thought about my mother packing a small case with some of my clothes, leaving behind all my pretty dresses, hair slides, shoes and toys for my sisters who were to remain in Carriacou.

I frowned as I thought about how unfair that was, but then decided maybe my mother had lots of pretty dresses waiting for me when we landed.

I sat up a little straighter and looked out the cabin window as the plane began to descend. Judith and I held on tightly to each other's hands. My stomach leapt in protest, I was sure my tummy was trying to come out of my mouth. A striking pain suddenly filled my ears, it was as if my head wanted to explode. And then with a thud, we had landed. Judith and I breathed a sigh of relief and hurriedly gathered our things and stood by our Mother.

The aeroplane door opened, and a gust of cold air filled the cabin. I had never felt cold like it before, except on my hands when Mama gave me an ice cube. It felt like I had walked into a fridge. Not even the blankets the stewardess wrapped around me could shield from the bitter air. I could still smell the vomit on my dress, and as I breathed in, the air bit the inside of my nose. I pulled the blanket around my face in an attempt to stop the chill.

I looked around wide-eyed as we walked into the huge airport. It was so much bigger than where we had boarded the plane. Our little legs struggled as we pulled the bags and suitcases, until we found a seat and huddled together to keep warm. My mother looked perplexed as we sat and waited. She didn't say anything, but kept looking around agitated, like she was expecting someone. It was an hour since we had arrived and Pamela's crying was relentless. Judith and I were freezing and desperately wanted to sleep, but we tried our best to stay awake, sitting silently so as not to get in the way. We watched the people hurrying past with suitcases all dressed in warm looking coats. Every time someone walked through the double doors, a gust of cold air would come in. We shuddered and I buried my head into Judith's shoulder. Eventually my mother stood up as two men came towards us. She greeted the first man. He was white, but red-faced from the cold, and wore a heavy coat that zipped up to his chin and a woolly hat with a pompom on the top. His face was round and friendly.

"Hello girls, I'm Uncle Harry," he said, taking off his gloves as he bent down and shook our hands. "You must be very cold. Don't worry, we will have you warm in no time." He smiled and turned to my mother apologising for their lateness. The other man was a little shorter than my mother. He was dark-skinned with a black moustache and big eyes. He too wore a hat, but it didn't have a pompom and it wasn't woolly. His knee-length coat was black with buttons and he wore a scarf hung loosely around his neck. The break in his coat collar showed a white shirt and a blue and black striped tie. My mother turned to him and frowned.

"What kept you so long? The children are cold and hungry," she said irritated. The man took out two pairs of shoes and woolly tights from a bag and told me and Judith to put them on. My mother handed Pamela to him taking the bag. She took us into the toilet to change into the clothes which felt heavy and restrictive, but they were warm. We emerged tightly clad in a hat, scarf and gloves. When we got back to the seats, the other man handed my mother a flask with soup, which she poured into plastic cups and told us to drink it. Judith nudged me and pulled a face. The soup really didn't taste very nice, but we were hungry and it warmed our grumbling stomachs.

The journey to where we were to live was long and we had to stop a few times, as the soup I drank earlier erupted like a volcano out of my stomach. It was dark when we arrived at the house. I opened my eyes to find I was being carried down a dimly lit corridor that smelt of fried food, which made my stomach heave again. I was eventually laid on a bed next to Judith who was already fast asleep. My mother left me in my coat and took off my shoes covering me with a blanket. The room was cold and damp and the light was as dim as the one in the corridor. I fell asleep to hushed voices, the rumble of suitcases and the rustle of bags.

The next morning I woke up to children's voices and for a split moment I thought I was home with Mama, but the reality was far from what I had left behind. Instead of waking up to light sheets and the warm air of Carriacou, I was buttoned up in a coat and covered in a thick blanket, and through it I could still feel the cold. I put my hands to my nose, trying to block out the thick smell of damp and a strange burning smell that I didn't recognise. *I am brave, I am brave.* I put one foot out of the bed and felt the cold, threadbare carpet through my tights.

"No, no, no. Put these slippers on, you'll make yourself ill from this floor," my mother said, so I stood up and slid my feet into the warmth of the furry slippers.

"You see that there," my mother pointed towards a long cylinder in the middle of the room, "it's a paraffin heater, and you are not to touch it, you hear?" I nodded in obedience, and watched as my Mother returned to it. She was pouring some hot water from a saucepan that had been balancing on the heater. I had never seen anything like it before. It was the cause of the awful smell, but I was glad it was there, as it was the only source of warmth in the room. My mother poured the warm water into a bowl and signalled for me to come.

"There are too many people using the bathroom, so you will have to wash here." She handed me a flannel and a bar of soap and left me to wash. I shivered as I started to undress. *I wish Myrtle was here to help me.*

"No, no! Don't strip off like that. Do your face and arms first, dry them and put your top on, then work your way down," she said frantically, "you'll catch a cold."

I wondered what she meant by 'catch a cold' it sounded like something not to be caught even if someone kindly threw it at you, so I did as I was told. She handed Judith the callboy kettle.

"Go to the kitchen and fill that up with water." Judith took the kettle and obediently did as she was asked.

There wasn't much to do so Judith and I sat together on our bed waiting for our next instruction. The kettle started to whistle, calling for attention.

"That must be why they call it 'callboy'- it calls you when it's boiled!" I thought out loud. Judith looked at me and burst out laughing.

"Yes silly. What do you think?" I cut my eye at her as she went over to where Pamela was sitting and made funny faces to make her laugh. My mother prepared Milo with the water from the kettle and buttered bread, carefully cutting it and placing it on a plate. The green and white Milo tin reminded me of home. I closed my eyes and pictured Mama stirring in the sweet chocolate granules into a saucepan of fresh goat's milk. My mother's voice broke into my thoughts.

"Come on you two. Breakfast is ready." I climbed down from the bed and followed Judith. My mother handed each of us a plate. "Sit at that table there." She pointed to a small wooden table and two chairs in the corner of the room. Even the chair was cold, in fact the bread and jam was too. *This doesn't look like breakfast,* I thought, picking up a slice of bread and biting into it. *Where's the saltfish and cabbage? Where's the fried plantain and bakes?* I looked at Judith and she shrugged her shoulders as if she had read my mind. She put her finger to her lips telling me not to talk. My mother put two cups of Milo in front of us.

"Drink it before it gets cold." She left us and went across the room to Pamela. *Yuck!* The Milo tasted nothing like we had at home, but we didn't dare protest, instead we sat and ate in silence.

Later that day, I watched my mother as she cooked our simple meal on the paraffin heater. The meat was cooked first, and then she would add water, rice and vegetables into the same pot and cover it. She bent down and turned a little knob on the side of the heater until the flame went down, leaving the food to cook.

"Come on you two, I need some help to clean up this place." My mother's words sounded like music to my ears. I had been sitting down watching her for so long, I was glad to be able to do something. I jumped off the bed and hurried to where she was standing. She handed me a cloth and a small bowl of warm water.

"Wipe down this wood all around here. Don't worry about the bits you can't reach," she instructed pointing to the fireplace. "Come on Judith. Put on your coat, we are going outside to wash that dirty window." She helped Judith with her coat, hat and scarf and they both went outside. I was relieved it wasn't me going out in the cold.

The fireplace wasn't easy to clean, with all its carved curvy wood and it was hard to see all the dust on the dark polished surface which seemed to add to the dreariness of the room. I leaned my hand on the wall to steady myself as I worked. The wall was so cold I shuddered and quickly removed it. I stopped for a while taking in the decor of the cramped space that had now become our home. The walls were covered in pink and green floral paper, which was worn and faded. My mother tied a string across the room and draped a sheet over to separate our beds from theirs for privacy. There was no picture of my family that I could look at to ease the ever growing yearning for my Mama. Coming to England and living with strangers, in such a cramped space, with no place to play, and without my precious family, meant only one thing... I was being punished. I decided that my mother brought me here as punishment for loving Mama more than her. There was no other reason. Earlier that day I asked her when I was going back home. She looked me in the eyes and said,

"This is your home now, so you will just have to get used to it." She was resolute. I quietly walked away and sat in the corner by the bed, hurriedly wiping away the tears from my eyes. I didn't want her to know that I was crying, but most of all I didn't want to let Mama down.

"This won't be forever," I thought to myself as I walked over to the window. Standing on my tiptoes, I peered out and watched Judith and my mother as they splashed water and chatted. Even though Pamela was asleep on the bed, a feeling of loneliness crept over me.

"I am brave!" I said out loud causing Pamela to stir. "I am brave," I whispered. Sighing deeply, I went back to cleaning the fireplace.

Yes you are brave and courageous.

I turned around to see if Pamela had spoken, but she was still fast asleep.

"This place even has speaking walls," I said to myself. I closed my eyes. I wasn't here in this awful house, I was a Princess locked in a tall tower. I was wearing the most beautiful dress that Mama had obviously made. I was surrounded by beautiful things, and my jailors, well they were frauds, pretending to be my parents. But I knew, the truth, I had been kidnapped and my real parents would come for me any minute, climb up that tall tower and rescue me! I opened my eyes and giggled. This had become my favourite fantasy and I was sure one day it would come true. One day I would return to the Queen, my real mother, my Mama, and I would be rescued from this dingy place. I spun around delicately, and then looked back at the fireplace. *Huh,* maybe I was

Cinderella instead. *Cinderella scrub the floors, Cinderella make the beds.* I giggled as I thought back to how we used to pretend back home, acting out the stories Myrtle would tell us. I was missing Becca and Dana - it felt like we had been separated for such a long time. Maybe they were good and didn't have to come to this dark, cold place, where everyone looked unhappy and the sun hardly ever shone.

Judith and my mother returned and she set about getting dinner ready.

"Judith, take that bowl of water from Beth and throw it down the drain I just showed you." Judith quickly did as she was told. She returned and took her coat and hat off.

"Look at my hands Beth," her fingertips were completely white. She chased me around the room trying to put her cold hands on me. I screamed every time she caught me.

"Stop it you two! What did I say about running around?" My mother's voice rose to an angry pitch. We both stopped immediately, frozen to the spot. "If you knock down that heater the place would catch on fire, then you would have to sleep outside in the cold. Is that what you want?" Her eyes flashed with fear, glistening with tears as she placed the plates on the table.

"No Mum, sorry," we both chorused. Unsure of whether to move around the room at all, I looked up at Judith for direction. She signalled to the bed and we both slowly walked over and sat down. The raised voices woke Pamela. My mother quickly walked across the room and picked her up, hushing her as she rocked her back to sleep.

"Go and sit at the table and eat your food," she said quietly. We both sat and ate our food in silence, not daring to speak another word. We had never seen her so angry before.

A few weeks later, I woke up to Judith's excited voice.

"Look Beth, manna has fallen from heaven!" I jumped out my bed and looked out the window and, sure enough the ground was covered in something white. Judith and I quickly dressed and ran to the front door, but we were abruptly stopped by my mother before we had the chance to open it.

"Where are you two going?" Her voice was firm.

"Manna has fallen from heaven and we just want to see it," Judith said anxiously. My mother smiled. It was the first time I saw her smile since we arrived.

"Come and get your coats on." We both ran back to the room and quickly got our coats, and ran towards the front door. "Ah! Come back, don't forget your hat and gloves," she said handing Judith her scarf and putting mine around my neck. She opened the door and we both looked out in amazement. "That's not manna," she chuckled. "It's called snow. Pick it up and you will see." We forgot about the icy air as we scooped up the snow. It was freezing and melted in our hands leaving our gloves soggy and wet. I put some in my mouth just to taste it.

"No don't eat it, you'll get sick," my mother said quickly, "spit it out!" I spat, but it had already melted in my mouth. Shaking her head, she turned and went back inside, leaving us by ourselves for the first time. There was snow everywhere, even the rooftops were covered in it.

"Look Judith, the roof has something sticking out of it!"

"Mum said they are chimneys. People light fires in the house and the smoke comes through them, so the houses don't get smoky."

"Oh! Why would they light fires in the house?" I asked curiously as I thought back to my mother's fear of the room catching on fire.

"You know that fireplace you cleaned?"

"Um hum."

"They light the fire in there to keep warm," she said walking up and down leaving her footprints in the crisp snow. I stood looking at the houses all joined together and decided they looked like a prison. There was no front yard and no grass to play ball. However the snow decorated the few trees and when you looked up the street, you couldn't tell where the road ended and the path began. It was picture perfect, like the postcards Mama used to get.

"You're new here, aren't you?" a boy came up to us with a ball of snow in his hand. I stayed behind Judith as they spoke.

"Yes," she replied.

"Do you want a snowball fight?"

"What's a snowball fight?"

"You roll the snow like this," he showed Judith twisting and turning the snow in his hand, "then you have to throw it at someone, but you mustn't let them catch you back," he explained.

"Ok," Judith gathered up some snow in her hands and rolled it into a ball and threw it. She laughed and ran around dodging the other children's snowballs. I joined in laughing and screaming, but every time a snowball hit me it hurt and I decided I didn't like the game. Just as I turned to call Judith, a snowball came whizzing through the air and hit me right in my face. I screamed out in pain as the icy ball stung my skin. I tried not to cry, but the sensation brought instant tears to my eyes. Judith came running over to me and moved my hands away to examine my face.

"Oh no! It's marked your face!" she said putting her arms around me. "Come on, I better take you to Mum."

Coming in from the bright white snow of outside, and the lively laughter we had left, made the room look darker and more silent than ever before. I removed my wet gloves and coat as Judith explained to my mother what had happened. She didn't comment, just got a flannel, gently wiped my face and put cream on it.

Although I didn't like snowball fights, I decided that I liked snow. It made the dull grey skies and dirty dark houses look clean and bright. For the first time since I got off the plane, I had laughed and played.

I soon realised that my father was the dark-skinned, formally dressed man that came to the airport with Uncle Harry to meet us, when we arrived in England. He wasn't as tall as the men in my family back home, but he was tall enough for my mother. I thought he was handsome especially when he smiled, which he didn't do very often. His eyes seemed to grow really big when he got cross, which made him look scary. He was always dressed in a shirt and tie, even when he was at home. I didn't really get to know him, because he was rarely with us and when he was, we had to be really quiet and not disturb him, which was difficult living altogether in one room. He was a preacher and travelled extensively so we spent most of our time with our mother. He didn't talk to us except to give us an order and he never said, "thank you" or smiled when we accomplished the task, which made the environment tense and uncomfortable.

This room we now called home was not permanent. We moved several times from one rented room in a house to another. The last move was a little different because we had an addition to the family - our baby brother was born. He was gorgeous with lots of straight black hair and chubby cheeks. This time my parents rented two rooms, one downstairs for them and one upstairs for us. My mother appeared more settled at this house. She began to draw me in with her kind, softly spoken voice. I noticed her dark eyes always looked sad even when she smiled. I can't remember her ever laughing out loud. When my father was away from home, her discipline was firm but gentle. In fact she behaved very similar to Mama. She very rarely went to midweek services at church, because she said we were too young to be left by ourselves and she didn't want to leave Pamela and Daniel with strangers. I remember my father being very upset about this. However, it was in this house that I was to have my first personal encounter with this person, who would later become so precious to me.

Chapter 3
Hello

Weeks turned into months and months into years and before I knew it, three years had passed. The eight year old me, was still convinced that back home in Carriacou was where I belonged. England was still not home for me and the more I fixated, the more Carriacou and Mama became a flawless, picture-perfect and far away fantasy.

Life in England wasn't all bad. My rich black hair had grown past my shoulders, and Mum had taught me the benefits of the pressing comb. I would sit by the gas cooker and cringe as the red hot comb pulled through my curly thick hair, straightening any kinks. And then she would cut it into a style that made me feel all grownup. School was a different story. Nobody liked that my hair swished this way and that - the white girls touched it with curiosity, while the black girls eyed me with suspicion. They made it clear I was not one of them.

"Coconut," they called me, implying I was not black enough to be part of their group. No, I did not like school - I avoided it at all costs.

On this occasion I wasn't escaping school, instead I was curled up in my bed, struggling to breathe. My chest tightened, I took a deep breath trying not to cough. The pain was so intense that I wrapped my hands around my stomach, rocking as tears seeped from my closed eyes.

Glancing over at my bedside table, there lay the envelope, marked with a Carriacou stamp, the letter it had contained scrunched up beside it. I closed my eyes tightly again as I remembered that 'it' was the reason I was in bed right now, too ill to move. Becca had written me for the first time. She wrote about home, about school, about my family, and told me about new friends she had made. They weren't our friends they were hers, and I was here, without any. I should've been with her, we were twins, we should have been together. My chest wheezed again, as my body screamed out the emotional pain I was in. I had excitedly scanned the letter looking for where Mama's name had appeared. And there it was - she had sent her love. She loved me, of course she loved me, she was my Mama, and she hadn't forgotten about me. And that's when it happened - suddenly I couldn't breathe, I couldn't speak, I was fighting for breath. I needed to be home, I needed to be with her, with them. I crumpled to the floor, holding the letter to my chest, sobbing uncontrollably.

Mum had come into the room, having heard the thud as I fell to the floor. She had found me gasping for air, paralysed. She called the doctor and I was rushed to him. He had said that I had an asthma attack. He had asked me if I was exerting myself at the time, and I had to answer honestly. I explained that I had received a letter from home and then suddenly I couldn't breathe. He smiled sympathetically at me and turned to my mother. He advised her that the cause of the asthma was my unhappiness, that I was homesick and that she should send me back to my family in Carriacou. But true to form, she refused to discuss it and would not even talk about our life back home. Instead the subject was changed, and my grief ignored. It may have been her way of protecting me, but to me, it was another way of her punishing me. She never hit me, she never shouted, it was the silence. She simply refused to speak about any of it.

And so here I was, in bed, desperation bringing tears to my eyes again, and before long I was sobbing into my knees. The pain in my chest was becoming unbearable, and I'd had enough of suffering. I rolled onto my back, heaving and convulsing, struggling to breathe.

"Please, help me," I wheezed, tears rolling down my cheeks. "Mama said you would take care of me. So where are you? She's not here, I need you," I pleaded, the tears sending me into a coughing fit. I don't know why I bothered, I didn't even know who I was talking to. Not really. It was then that I heard a gentle voice.

Beth

I opened my eyes and looked towards my bedroom door. There was no one in my room. But there was that voice again, *where did it come from?* I dropped my head back down on my pillow.

"I'm going crazy, I'm hearing voices. They put people like me in hospital for sure."

Beth.

It was clear this time, audible. I wasn't going crazy, someone was speaking to me. I laughed to myself, *I'm like Samuel, in the Sunday school story.* If the story was to be believed, then I should have responded and said, "Lord here I am." But I didn't believe in fairy-tale stories, and I wasn't convinced that the stories my father forced me to read in the mornings were relevant to my life. I mean it would have been great if they were true, maybe then my Mum could be convinced to send me back to Mama.

I'm right here.

Umhmm I heard that. I have no intention of responding, and becoming like Samuel. Living in a church with a minister controlling me and not letting me go back home. No, church is not the place for me, I am living that nightmare already. I had seen the minister's life, the fake smiles even when you are crying inside. I had learnt to conceal my feelings all for the façade of church, pretending to be someone I was not. I'm going to sleep. I rolled over and closed my eyes tight.

Silence.

He had stopped speaking. *Had I offended Him?* Maybe He was kind and loving like my Mama. I had heard this voice before. It always seemed to speak to me when I was upset or sick. There were times in the night when it sounded like someone was singing over me, as I cried myself to sleep. Other times it felt as though my head was being stroked, as I lay on the couch gasping for breath. But this time it felt real like He was right there, crouched down near to me.

"Ok, I'm sorry. Are You still here?"

Silence.

Beth, I am here.

He knew me by name. This was weird.

Come.

And suddenly I could see Him, clearly. He was not just handsome, but beautiful. He had soft kind eyes, which seemed to see straight into my heart. His lips and skin colour reminded me of Mama. He stretched out His hand.

Come.

I reached up and took His hand. Ok, I was in a dream, this was not happening. *I'm holding the hand of...who? Whose hand was I holding?* Mum had warned me not to go with strangers, but this was different. I was still in my bed, but I wasn't. I could see Him, He was there in my room. Then suddenly I wasn't in my room anymore.

He led me through a wooden door, the shape of a heart that opened into a garden. I gasped in awe. I was standing on soft, emerald green grass in the prettiest garden I had ever seen. It was covered in beautiful flowers arranged in neat flower beds, and in the middle of the garden was a fountain. The water sprayed up and then flowed into a lily pond. He led me to a wooden bench, very much like the one my Uncle had made in our garden back home. He sat down, and beckoned me to come next to Him. I looked at Him wearily.

"Who are you?" It was a little late to be asking Him this, but nevertheless, He didn't look like the Bible story characters I had read about. He didn't seem angry like the Man who was spoken about from the pulpit on a Sunday.

"I am Jesus."

"Oh really." I slowly sat down next to Him.

"Would you like to help me plant some flowers?" I nodded and followed Him to the other side of the garden. "The seasons are changing so we need to plant some new flowers." He smiled as He handed me a pair of pink wellington boots. They were a perfect fit. He then gave me a small trowel and showed me how to dig the hole and plant the seeds.

"Are you the person Mama said would take care of me?" I asked.

"Always, Beth, I will always take care of you, if you let me."

"I want to go home, to my Mama. Where do you live?"

"I live with my family."

I listened to Him as He talked about His Father, "You'll love Him Beth. When you know me you will know Him, we are so much alike. He's kind and gentle, but strong and mighty to protect those He loves. He loves children. He even knows how many hairs are on your head."

"Why would He want to know that?" I shook my

fringe that fell by my eyes, trying to imagine someone counting each strand.

"Because you are so important to Him. On the day you were born and given your name, He wrote it on the palm of His hands - you are so precious to Him. He is very creative and has wonderful plans for your life, just you wait and see."

His face beamed with joy which made Him appear like a glowing light. I longed to have a father like His who really loved and cared about me. The more time we spent together, the more I became dependent on Him and wanted to be with Him. He became my escape from the loneliness I felt. I missed the flower gardens back home. It was so compassionate and thoughtful of Him to invite me into His garden every time I needed to talk to Him, so that we could spend quiet times together.

Years passed and before I knew it, I had begun to accept British life. Memories of Carriacou were put on a pedestal and, I determined in my heart that I would reach back there as soon as I was old enough. These dreams seemed to sustain me, as I managed the battlefield of senior school. I lived my teenage years much like my mother had taught me, speak little of your thoughts, be dignified and do what is expected of you to keep peace with people. I was fourteen years old now and so the garden had become more of a childish dream I had once participated in. It wasn't that I had forgotten any of its beauty, but I knew that believing such things would not help me fit in. I was still a Christian, and I could still see Jesus, in the little things. I would pray quietly in my mind, asking Him to help me, and I would feel an overwhelming sense of peace. But it had become harder to see Him as I had done before – it was no longer simple and uncomplicated. The church had taught me so much, "doctrine" they called it - lots of rules of how to live to be accepted by Jesus. Faith had become confusing. Believing, and simply seeing Jesus, could not possibly be enough, *could it?*

Life at home had changed and the atmosphere became even more tense and unbearable. I was fourteen years old and was experiencing the effects of my silence. It had been mistaken for timidity and I was presumed vulnerable. For the past year, two men were abusing their place of trust and their affections intensified. They were like rats coming from the garden into the house every time my parents went out. No one had ever treated me like this before and I wasn't really sure how to make it stop. I hated it. It made me feel dirty and worthless. I was fed up of scratching, biting and fighting, so I wrote them a letter telling them in no uncertain terms to leave me alone. I was growing up now becoming a woman; I didn't have to put up with this anymore. When I finished writing, I carefully put the letter in an envelope and placed it on my dressing table, so that I didn't forget to post it on my way to school the next day. I lay on my pillow satisfied that I had done the right thing. If they had any doubt about my feelings towards their unwanted attention, then this would surely clear things up. Morning came all too quickly and I hurried out the house and forgot my precious letter.

"Why didn't you put it in your bag?" I scolded myself on the way to school that morning, but it was too late to go back and get it. For the whole day, I tried hard to store it at the back of my mind, telling myself that I would post it later.

After school, I ran all the way home, my heart beating hard and questions racing through my head - what if Mum went into my room and found the letter. The men's voices echoed in my mind,

"You better not say anything," they taunted, "You know your father would beat you if he found out."

No he would protect me! I screamed in my head fighting back the fear as I ran faster, trying not to listen to their voices. I raced into the house and up the stairs pausing on the banister. My fears were now magnified. It was Friday afternoon and my father came home earlier than usual.

"Look at this," there was silence, "I found it in Beth's room." I strained to hear what was being said, but it wasn't long before I clearly heard my father's deep raised voice.

"What kind of nonsense is this?" he growled in anger as he spoke. "These children of yours behave like this because you are too soft on them," he was shouting and my heart was pounding.

"What do you mean my children? They are your children too!" I had heard my mother shout before, but not at my father. "They are only my children when they have done something wrong. Anyway you need to sort it out and maybe if you were home more often..." He didn't let her finish her sentence.

"Don't put your guilt trip on me. You wanted them, you look after them." There were heavy footsteps and a door slammed. I wanted to hide but there was nowhere safe enough. I shuddered as I heard my father talking on the phone. He ordered the two men to whom the letter was addressed to to come to the house right away. I quietly crept to my room and sat curled up on my bed awaiting my fate. I didn't like what he had said to my mother. I was in no doubt that he didn't care about me now, he had not really wanted me. His actions were clear from the first day I met him. *What if he doesn't believe what's written in the letter?* I felt sick, my mouth dry from panic as I rocked backward and forward waiting.

It wasn't long before I was summoned to the lounge where the men sat in a row. My father held my precious letter in his hands, waving it at me as he demanded to know what it was about. He didn't give me a chance to defend myself and after a barrage of questions with no opportunity for me to give an answer, he ordered that I apologise to the men. I looked at them sitting there like rats, their long tails curled around them, their whiskers twitching in anticipation, then I said in a defiant voice,

"No, I won't apologise to them, they know the truth."

Their jaws dropped open. My father's eyes grew wide in anger and humiliation. These men held important positions in the church, and his daughter was now compromising not only their integrity, but also his. I stared back at him unflinching. The two men were about to defend themselves when my father put out his hands to silence them.

"What did you say?!" unbuckling his belt he looked straight into my eyes, his eyes flashed with anger, his voice booming through the room.

I didn't dare repeat what I said. He was furious. I had spoken; I had opened my mouth and told the truth. I couldn't back down now. *How could he defend them, how could he take their side over mine?* So I stood my ground and braced myself for the consequences of my defiance.

He pulled the black leather belt from their loops, lifted my skirt and struck me. The pain coursed through my body causing my eyes to spring water. I gritted my teeth and fought back the tears. I couldn't cry in front of these abusers and let them win again. As another blow came down on my back, I held my breath, stiffened my body and shut my eyes, squeezing back the tears. My father's voice broke into my thoughts.

"So you think you are hard, do you? You think you are bigger than me!" Another blow came down on my legs. I thought I was going to pass out. No one had ever hit me before and I reeled from the pain.

"Get out of my sight!" he growled as he pushed me out the room, incensed that he hadn't reduced me to tears. My mother didn't come and rescue me from my torture; she didn't even put out her hands to catch me as my father pushed me out the door. I only saw the back of her head as she turned and disappeared through the kitchen door.

I ran up to my bedroom and buried my head into my pillow, muffling my screams as my body trembled in pain, my mind replaying every blow my father landed on my body. It wasn't just the physical pain I felt, it was the humiliation and rejection that stung the most.

"Jesus, help me!" I shouted into my pillow. I needed Him to come and take me into the garden like He did when I was younger, but Jesus didn't come, He didn't seem to hear me. My father had lifted my skirt, exposed me in front of my abusers, the more I thought about it the more I cried. *How could I ever trust him again!* Those men knew my father better than I did and now my fight would start all over again. I was disgraced and betrayed, and Jesus appeared to desert me just when I needed Him most.

The respect for my father from that day on was out of duty, the little relationship we had, dissolved. For me, my home and the church were not safe places anymore. I couldn't even depend on my mother for protection. I went to church because I had no choice - this was my father's rule and it had to be obeyed. I became the Sunday School Coordinator, I led the services, sang songs and even prayed the way I was expected to, despite the fact it didn't mean anything to me. I became a brilliant actress, who knew the script and could pass any church audition. But my heart was aching; I needed to get away from church and home to a safe place.

I had often contemplated going into the garden and a few times Jesus would surprise me as He showed up there right in front of me. He would remind me of how much

He loved me, but I just couldn't accept it.

"Jesus I can't do this!" I was struggling to trust Him. I didn't have the strength to have a relationship with Him.

"Beth I know you can't, but I can. Let me do this for you." His voice was earnest and I wanted to believe Him, but I couldn't. *Where was He when I needed Him most?*

"I'm sorry Jesus. I don't mind remaining friends, but nothing more." His eyes were moist with tears as He held my hand in His.

"Beth, I will never stop loving you. I will wait for you." He released my hands and I turned and walked away from Him. I couldn't understand why He wanted a relationship with me anyway. I didn't feel good enough for Him, I felt rejected, dirty and used. What would His Father say if He knew who His Son was hanging out with?

Love, He loved me...well I no longer wanted the love that was inflicted on me by men. I was determined that no one would ever hurt me again. I had broken my silence, I had spoken out, and I had not been believed, I had not been protected. But I had found a power in not crying when I had been beaten. It had given me a strength inside – it had hidden all my emotions, all my feelings, all the pain, disgrace and rejection inside me. That power felt like steel that no one could penetrate. And by not showing emotion, and hardly laughing, I had an armour - I would protect myself.

I was nearly sixteen when my sisters came to England.

They looked so different, all grown up and elegant. Becca, my twin sister and I were the same height, black shoulder length hair and same slim build. It was strange looking at someone almost identical to me. Our personalities clashed at first, because I felt like I had lost my identity as the adults insisted on comparing us continually. We were no longer Beth and Becca, but 'Twinny'. Dana was a year younger than me. She had smooth dark skin, perfectly set eyes and black hair. Everyone said she was the most stunning of the sisters and they were not wrong, because she was beautiful like my mother.

I thought about Mama and how she must have felt losing two more children. I hadn't allowed myself to think about her for a while. I buried those thoughts and emotions years before, so the thought came without warning. I quickly tucked it back down inside me. Thankfully Becca and Dana didn't often talk about their life back home. My memories of a child didn't match up with the reality they felt of being left behind. They wanted their Mum, I wanted my Mama.

Chapter 4
Escape

I didn't go to college after leaving school. I got a job working at a local Day Nursery. It had been two years and I was ready for a change. It wasn't that the job wasn't interesting or I didn't get on with the staff. Working with children was rewarding and every day posed a different challenge. Hearing them say a new word, grow new teeth or take their first step was fulfilling. It was more the need to get away from the 'non-existence' of me. I didn't want to be the unfeeling unemotional robot that I had become. I wanted a change of environment, but I didn't have enough money to go abroad, my mother saw to that. I was expected to give her my pay packet every week and from that she gave me pocket money. I was almost nineteen and I wanted to control my own money. I wanted my own space and to make my own choices. All my sisters except Pamela and I had left home. I felt a sense of responsibility for her and didn't want to leave her by herself, but I had to do something, I needed space to stretch and to breathe. There had to be more to life than this mundane existence. I didn't want to live pleasing everyone else, I wasn't a child anymore. My sisters were well-educated and all had qualifications that would enable them to get good jobs, but I didn't. My medical and school records caused a few raised eyebrows when I had applied for jobs after leaving school, so I should have been grateful for the one I had. It wasn't that I wasn't grateful, it just wasn't enough anymore.

A new job and a new home seemed to be my only hope - my escape from my father's constant reminder that he didn't want me in his house, my mother's sadness and the heavy, depressing atmosphere of the house. And most of all the church. Living on my own would mean I wouldn't have to attend, I could choose whether I wanted to or not. The garden no longer existed for me, it was always there in the back of my mind, but I needed reality. I had convinced myself that the garden and Jesus were not important in my life, not now.

I went into the staffroom for my break as usual and sat talking to my friend Marie. She was looking for a job too, but she wanted to go to London to be nearer to her family, and I was looking for one to get away from mine. We both scanned the noticeboard.

"Ah well, doesn't look like there is anything here for me," she sighed, sitting down and sipping her tea.

"I think I've found something! Come and have a look!" Marie and I stood close together in order to read at the same time. "Am I reading it right?" There on the notice board was an advert for a Nursery Nurse at a residential nursery working with babies and children. It came with a bedsit in a Tudor style house, with well-maintained grounds.

"It's only in Handsworth Wood you know," Marie smiled, a half- hearted smile. I could hear from her tone that she wasn't really too excited about me finding something. She had been looking to leave this job a lot longer than me.

"Yes that's perfect," I replied writing down the information.

"But is that far away enough for you?" she frowned, attempting to find flaws in the position. She sat down and picked up her cup, cautiously.

"Well, it would be a start." I sat next to her and sipped my tea, "Ewh it's gone cold."

"And you would be working with children again," she informed me like I hadn't noticed.

I sighed deeply and said slowly, "Yes Marie, I can read you know, and anyway I enjoy working with children."

"Then go for it." She sounded a little more upbeat, but deep down I knew she was worried about me leaving her.

"At least we wouldn't be too far from each other. You could visit me after work," I smiled reassuringly as we washed our cups and she promised not to tell anyone until I was sure I had the job.

"You sound like you've already got the job," she nudged me in my ribs and laughed out loud.

"I believe in faith and hope," I said drying my hands. I

don't know why I said that, it just seemed to come out of nowhere.

"Go you! It seems like you are learning something from that church you go to after all. Maybe I should come with you one Sunday." She was serious.

Her comment threw me off guard and I struggled to respond. I had never invited anyone to church. How could I invite my friend to a place that caused me so much grief and pain? A place I hated going to! How could I introduce my friend to a minister who was one thing at church and another at home? I had never told her my father was the leader of the church. In fact I didn't talk about my life at home at all, she wouldn't have understood coming from a family that loved her.

"Okay, I'll take you up on that one Sunday," I tried to sound as positive as I could, but the words stuck in my throat.

"Are you ok?" she frowned as I coughed.

"Yes I'm ok," I hung up the towel and smiled, "Come on, we'll be late back."

From that day I was careful not to say anything that would cause the subject of church to come up in conversation. I was becoming everything I didn't like most about church - a fraud, living one principle inside the church, and another outside.

Two days later the application form for the Nursery Nurse post arrived. I sat in my bedroom and filled it in right away. I held the large envelope close to my chest as I walked to the post-box at the end of the street. I wanted to pray over it, but I hadn't spoken to Jesus for a while, so instead I looked up to the sky and dropped the precious letter into the post-box.

At last, I was invited for an interview. I was so excited I booked the day off work and took the bus to Handsworth Wood. I didn't tell anyone about the interview, not even Marie. It was my planned escape and I wanted to make sure it went off without a hitch.

After the interview, I booked three weeks' holiday from work so I would be at home when the acceptance letter arrived. I paced up and down by the front door every morning, waiting with anticipation for the postman to click the letterbox and put me out of my misery. It became unbearable waiting day after day for the letter to arrive. I even cleaned every corner of my room in preparation. It didn't even cross my mind that I could receive a rejection letter. Two weeks passed and still no letter, the routine had become wearisome.

I was woken up one morning to the click of the letter box. I couldn't believe I had overslept. Pulling my dressing gown around me, I ran down the stairs and stopped short on the seventh step before the end. To my horror my father was by the front door with two letters in his hand. He had a habit of opening letters that were not addressed to him.

"If you don't like it then get your own letterbox," I remembered him saying one day, when I had been upset that my letter had disappeared mysteriously, and then resurfaced opened. I was trying my best not to despise him. The words 'Honour your father and mother,' kept me from answering back, but my tongue was getting sore from biting back my words.

"Please God if one of those letters is for me; please don't let him open it!" I whispered.

I held my breath as he swiftly moved one envelope on top of the other. My heart began to thump as he tore open the first envelope and began to scan its contents. I couldn't chance him opening the second letter, so I slowly moved down the last few steps and asked as casually as I could,

"Is one of those for me?" He turned around and looked at me slightly startled by my presence. As he turned away, he stuck out the unopened envelope in my direction without acknowledging that I had even spoken.

"Thank you," I said calmly as I quickly took it from his grasp and ran back up the stairs to my room. I tore the envelope open and started to read. Skipping the formalities I got to the part that I had been waiting for two weeks and three days.

> '...it gives me great pleasure to inform you that you have been successful in your application for the Nursery Nurse position. Please confirm your acceptance by way of post or by contacting...'

I had the job and I was elated! I fell back on my bed hugging my precious letter. I could breathe again.

After confirming my acceptance, I told my mother about the job and that I needed to live on the premises and would be starting at the end of the month. She didn't comment and I didn't volunteer any more information. I didn't say anything to my father, because he wasn't interested in anything I did or anywhere I went anyway. It was only last week that he had told me that I needed to find my own place to live. He didn't tell me why and I didn't question him.

My colleagues at work planned a leaving party for me with all the children and some of the parents. It was a lovely party and the older children sang a goodbye song from 'Sound of Music'. I laughed and hugged everyone, but felt no real emotion. I behaved in the way I was expected to behave, not in the way I really felt. Marie was happy for me, but because I didn't tell her about the interview, it put a strain on our relationship. Consequently, when she eventually got her job and moved to London, we didn't keep in touch.

At the end of the month I began packing my belongings like my life depended on it. I didn't want to leave anything behind. In my mind I was never coming back. Pamela sat on my bed watching while I packed. Her eyes were filled with tears. I stopped, sat next to her and put my arms around her. Her tears spilled down over her cheeks.

"I won't be far away, just a bus ride." I dried her eyes and kissed her forehead like Mama used to do to me.

"I can't get to you on the bus, so how would I see you?" Her little body shook with sobs.

"I'll come to see you and as soon as I've got enough money, I will learn to drive and get a car," I said trying to reassure her.

"But that will take ages!" She was not convinced.

"Don't worry Pam, we will work something out." I stretched across my bed, took my teddy bear and gave it to her. "Can you take care of him for me?" She hugged it and smiled.

"But he's your favourite."

"I know, but you can have him. Every time you miss me, give him a hug."

I continued packing as Pam and I talked. I gave her a few of my books and other precious belongings that I knew she liked. She watched my desperate packing and sighed, a deep sigh that seemed to echo from her heart, but I couldn't allow her emotions to interfere with this chance of escape.

On the final day, my Mum helped me pack the last box of odds and ends. To my surprise she gently placed her hand on mine.

"If the job doesn't work out, don't be afraid to come back home, your room will always be here, regardless of what your father says." I could see the tears welling up in her eyes that were already darkened with sadness. The last time I saw her looking like that was when she was in the kitchen back home, talking to Mama. She quickly turned away from my gaze and went to her room. She returned with two sheets and a pair of pillowcases still in their plastic wrappers, tied with a pink ribbon and handed them to me. She then handed me a small black box. "This is your grandmother's wedding ring. I want you to have it." She didn't look at me as she spoke. So many emotions ran through my head as she placed the gift in my hand. I couldn't find the right words to say anything that would make sense. I knew this must have been a difficult thing for her to do.

"Thank you." I threw my arms around her and held her tight. I wasn't expecting the tears that suddenly welled up in my eyes and rolled onto her shoulders. I couldn't remember ever embracing her in this way. My heart ached with her unhappiness, as she put her arms around me for the first time. It was as if she knew I could feel the heartbeat of her pain and quickly pulled away.

"Make sure you eat well and look after yourself, you know you and food aren't the best of friends." Her voice was shaky as she tried to conceal her feelings. She picked up the box filled with the last of my belongings and placed it in my hands. "Come on, take this box down to the car, you know how impatient your father can be." I took the box and looked back at her but she didn't look up.

"Thank you," I said blinking in an effort to hold back the tears that threatened to expose the tenderness I felt for her. Pam was at school so I walked down the corridor to her room. Putting down the box, I picked up my favourite teddy from her bed and hugged it for the last time.

"Look after her like you looked after me Mr Ted and give her this kiss for me." I placed him back on her bed, picked up the box and ran down the stairs.

My father had already started the engine, hurrying me like he had an important meeting to attend and I was making him late. It felt like he couldn't wait to get rid of me. The front seat was conveniently occupied with a large box so I sat at the back. I was relieved in a way, at least I didn't have to try and make conversation. Not a word was spoken and the fifteen minute journey felt like an hour, you could cut the atmosphere with a knife. My mother insisted on my father giving me a lift. I wished I had done as I had planned and taken a taxi. We turned into the long leafy drive with its trees towering above us. It looked quite dark, not as I had imagined and as the house came into view my heart missed a beat. It reminded me of a haunted house from a childhood story. My thoughts jolted back to reality as my father brought the car to a halt. He sat in the car, huffing and puffing, because I wasn't moving fast enough for him; without offering to help, he just watched me unload my belongings at the front step. He impatiently started up the car as I took the last suitcase out the boot and was ready to move off as I slammed it shut. There were no words of encouragement, no smile, and no goodbye. As the car disappeared down the drive I wanted to shout "I hate you!" but I didn't, I just stood frozen to the spot in disbelief.

It was early evening when I arrived. I shivered as I stood in front of the gigantic mansion with its huge black and white door and all my belongings at my feet. A cool summer breeze disturbed the trees as a gust of loneliness and fear blew over me. I shuddered as I fought back the fear and fumbled for the keys, silently scolding myself for allowing my emotions to get the better of me. Just as I turned the lock, I heard a bright cheery voice behind me.

"Hi, you must be Beth, I'm Annie," she said, putting her hand out. I took her hand and shook it in greeting.

"Sorry I'm late. Matron told me you were arriving today and I know how daunting it can be moving into a big place like this," she continued without stopping to breathe. "Come on then let's bring your things inside and I will show you where everything is."

A wave of relief washed over my fear as I thanked her. She showed me where the bedrooms, kitchen and bathrooms were on the ground floor, then we proceeded to the first and second floors. Her kind, smiling face put me at ease as she chatted away, unaware that she had not given me a chance to ask any questions.

After showing me around and giving me a history lesson of the house, we went downstairs to collect my belongings.

"Your room is on the first floor. You are lucky to have a bathroom next door to you," she informed me as we climbed the wooden stairs once again. We chatted as we went up and down the stairs a few times carrying my things, placing them down by my room door one by one. I put the last box down by my feet and leaned on the doorframe to catch my breath.

"There are so many stairs!"

"Ah, you'll get used to them," she laughed, "I'll go and give you a chance to settle in."

"Thank you so much for showing me around and for helping me carry all this stuff, I really appreciate it."

"No problem. Call me if you need me. I'm just down the corridor." I pushed my bedroom door open and peered in. It was massive!

"I could fit all four bedrooms of my father's house into

this one room!" I gasped in amazement. I stood in the doorway and took it all in. It was unbelievable, all this was mine - a high ceiling, beautiful covings and deep, dark oak coloured skirting boards that joined the dark polished wooden floors. There was a large, dark oak chest of drawers in the corner, with brass handles. Next to it was the most enormous wardrobe I had ever seen. Its dark wood dominated the room. I walked over and opened the doors to find that each door displayed its own long mirror held in place with gold fixtures. The dressing table was also made of dark wood, with a beautiful vanity mirror which stood delicately on carved legs. The king-sized bed was made of brass with a finely shaped metal floral design displayed on the head and foot board. The mattress looked deep and comfortable still covered in its plastic wrapper, which boasted it was brand new. In the middle of the room was a huge multi-coloured wool rug. There was a door in the corner which I thought would lead to a bathroom. I curiously walked over to take a look, but to my surprise, it was a kitchenette. There was no fridge or cooker, but there were cupboards and work surfaces, a sink and sockets for a kettle and toaster.

Walking back into the room, there was a musty smell which reminded me of the room we lived in when we first moved to England. I opened one of the five bay windows that overlooked the gardens to air the room. This gave me an enviable view of the beautiful grounds with its well-maintained lawns and lush flower beds surrounded by tall majestic trees. I couldn't see the road, but could hear the quiet hum of traffic, reminding me that

I was not far from the hustle and bustle of everyday life. You would think I was a hundred miles away somewhere in the countryside, but I was only a couple of miles from home. This was as far as I needed to go to get away from the sadness and the pain that my father's house represented.

I damp dusted the room and started unpacking my belongings. There in the corner of the last box was my Bible. It looked dog-eared and tired from its years of use. In the peace and tranquillity of my room, I sat in the armchair by the window and held it to my chest. Tears came from nowhere and I couldn't stop them. *Why on earth are you crying?* I angrily told myself.

This is what I had wanted, my own space, peace and quiet. I didn't have to walk on eggshells every time I emerged out of my room, not like at home. I should be elated, and yet here I was blubbering. I tucked my knees under my chin and rocked to the rhythm of my sobs. I held my breath in anger, trying to stop the tears from flowing, but they wouldn't cease. For the first time, I was alone. I felt like a child again sitting in a corner crying for my Mama. I was in this beautiful house with a great career ahead, but the realisation that this all depended on me was overwhelming. Frustrated, I irritably wiped the tears from my eyes. Then the thought flashed into my mind, *if I don't get this right, I'll have to go back home. I can't, no I can't go back there.* This is me, free, away from it all. So why could I feel the ache inside for the security of home?

Beth.

I quickly dried my eyes, composing myself as I slowly walked to the door. There was no one there.

"No, I am just tired and after all it has been a long day, I just need to get some sleep," I told myself. It was dark outside and I had completely lost track of the time. I drew the curtains and prepared for bed, still holding my Bible close to me. As I sunk into the thick blanket, the cool sheets made me shudder. I snuggled in burying my head under the covers. There I lay, propping up the blanket with my arm so I could open my Bible.

Beth.

I looked up and there was Jesus with His hands outstretched. My mouth went dry, my heart skipped a beat.

"Jesus! What are you doing here?" I said sitting up straight, allowing the blankets to fall around me.

"I heard you crying Beth, come with me to our special place," His voice was tenderly pleading. I took His hands and together we went into the garden. I didn't know what to say, but I felt a sense of peace I hadn't felt in a long time.

"I don't know if I can do this Jesus. I want to be here, I want this new experience, the freedom of being away from home. But it's scary, there's no one here to look after me. What if I've got it wrong?"

"Beth you are exactly where you should be. Why not let me help you?"

"You will, you will help me? I..I've been so angry at you Jesus," I admitted sheepishly, "I really don't deserve your help. It felt like you left me when I needed you most."

"I know you've been angry, but I've longed to see you. I would never ever leave you, even in the times when you are upset and you don't see me. I am always there."

"I'm so sorry, I don't understand how you could be so kind to me. Will you forgive me? I want this." I spun around looking at all the beauty of the garden, the peaceful tranquillity that filled me when I entered it. "I want this all the time, every day. It's so hard on my own. I really need your help."

"It sounds like you are asking me to be a part of your life." He asked beaming.

"Well, yes, yes I do want you to be."

He chuckled, "That is exactly what I wanted to hear. I would love to be in your life. You will never be alone again. There's so much I would love to tell you."

We continued to walk through the beautiful garden. I noticed that some of the flowers I had planted years before were now mature shrubs. Jesus continued to look after our garden even though I didn't go to meet Him there, and in my heart I questioned how I could have abandoned the love of the One who loved me most.

Chapter 5
Ouch

Not attending church was harder than I had thought it would be. I may have been living on my own, I may have had my own freedom, but I had been conditioned from a young age, and church was a permanent part of my life. I had friends there and choosing not to go, felt like another thing I would have to explain and apologise for. Getting to know Jesus, and attending the many services at church felt like two separate things - I felt like two different people. There was a freedom when I met with Jesus, I was loved unconditionally, and I could talk about anything. But at church I was still the world's best actress and I knew that I had to behave in a certain way to be accepted. I was a Pastor's Kid and that was exactly what was expected of me.

One Friday afternoon, I sat in church whilst the usual youth group crowd began to come in. There was a buzz of excitement as today we were practising a song, which was to be sung at a church service, that we were taking part in. We had decided that this service would be different, and so we had written songs, created drama skits and prepared a message which was clear and full of God's love.

The youth group leader called us all together at the front of the church on the stage. There were two new faces that I didn't recognise, and I knew everyone. Becca came up behind me, and whispered in my ear.

"See that guy over there," she motioned towards one of the new faces, "I've told him all about you, especially how you've got the same face as me," she playfully nudged into me. "He is eager to meet you!"

I blushed, "Becca don't be silly, I'm not interested." I turned away and followed the group leader's instructions. We all came together on the stage and began to sing. To my surprise, the nameless face had a beautiful voice. After rehearsals, Becca linked her arms in mine and informed me that she was taking me out.

"Out where?"

"Somewhere special and those two are coming along," she nodded to the two new faces and smiled brightly.

"Becca, you aren't serious, we don't even know them," I said exasperated, anchoring my feet to where I was standing.

"Well I know them both, they're my friends from college. Oh don't be boring Beth, you haven't been out with anyone in ages."

"Uh, I suppose," I rolled my eyes. Becca had a way of

convincing me around all the time. She was the more confident out of the two of us. I on the other hand would much prefer not to ruffle anyone's feathers. Becca knew what she wanted and would go for it. I envied her boldness sometimes, and conviction. I had moved out from home and still didn't know what I really wanted or what I believed. But Becca knew who she was and nothing and no one could dissuade her.

The guy's name was Duncan. I wasn't immediately attracted to him, but he had a soft manner and was very much a gentleman. I was nineteen and he was a year older than me. It wasn't long before we became good friends. We spent a lot of time together and it was constantly hinted that we were a perfect couple. No matter how many times I protested, and explained that we were just friends, I got raised eyebrows and a playful grin, as people presumed there was more than there actually was. We were friends, that was all, and I could handle that.

I had been complaining of recurring stomach pains that seemed to come and go. Then suddenly one afternoon, I was sitting in my bedroom and an overwhelming pain crunched into my stomach. I screamed out hugging myself tightly. Losing my balance, I fell off the chair and onto the ground.

Annie ran in frantically.

"Beth, what's happening, are you alright?" I couldn't respond, I was squirming on the floor in unbearable pain.

It wasn't long before the ambulance arrived and I was rushed into hospital. My appendix had burst and I had to have an operation to have it removed. The doctors insisted I move back home, to recuperate.

Being back, was hard, I was returning to everything I had escaped, everything I had left behind and vowed I would never return to. And it looked the same. My room, the house, the atmosphere, nothing had changed. My father was not happy that I had imposed on him.

"Remember this is only temporary. This is not your home anymore, you left." He reminded me with a stern voice.

"Yes Dad," I lowered my head. He didn't want me here, and I didn't want to be back here either. At least we agreed on something.

Duncan often came to visit me and brought me flowers. *How lovely of him,* I smiled looking at the vase filled with bright coloured roses. They seemed to brighten up the dullness of my room. A complete contrast to the disdain my father gave me. At least Duncan cared about me, at least he wanted me around. He made his affections clear, he wanted us to be in a relationship, in fact he wanted us to get married.

I lay on my childhood bed and thought about what I knew about love and marriage. Nothing, I knew nothing. I didn't know how I was supposed to feel about Duncan. I felt...I felt the familiar. We had gotten to know each other, and although my heart never raced and I didn't get the goose bumps that the TV heroines seemed to experience, I supposed I had a version of love. Maybe that was enough. *Could I tolerate Duncan?* Yes maybe I could. Anything was better than staying here in my father's house.

When Duncan and I got married, we moved five miles away to a beautiful newly built house. It had three bedrooms, one with a small veranda, where we often sat on a sunny afternoon, drank juice and watched the world go by. Like most couples, married life took some getting used to, but I wasn't expecting what was in store for me. I began to live in constant fear for my life as this calm, sweet-natured man turned into someone I didn't recognise. His beliefs turned into religion and he became fanatical, quoted scripture after scripture to try and correct the faults he felt I had as a Christian, and there were consequences if I didn't do as I was told.

I wanted our marriage to be different from the examples of marriage etched into my brain from childhood. I wanted us to sing and dance together, laugh and cry, have quiet times and crazy fun times like we had before we were married, but instead my lonely childhood days came crawling back. I was back in prison, being punished and I didn't know what crime I had committed. I became physically sick and lived in constant fear of doing or saying something wrong. My life was turning upside down and I was becoming silent like my mother, afraid to give my opinion, just agreeing for peace sake. Deep down inside of me I knew I had to do something, but I had no strength to fight and there was no one I trusted to help me.

My only peace came from going into the garden and

sitting with Jesus on the wooden bench that He had made for me. It was so restful there. The flowers were in full bloom and their fragrance had an intoxicating effect. Most days I didn't speak, my pain was too much to express in a few words. I just rested my head on His chest and cried, as He put His arms around my shoulder and cried with me. Other days, He just held me and hummed softly until I fell asleep.

I was isolated from the few friends I had and the new friends I made only came during day when Duncan went to work and left before he returned. He didn't want me sitting gossiping all day, it wasn't good for the soul, he told me. The children's home I worked at closed down after I had my first child, so I was out of work and Duncan now controlled the money that was coming into the house. When our second child was born, I knew I had to move closer to friends and family, just in case Duncan got over-zealous in the way he handled me. He was good with our children and looked after them, well when I was poorly, which was becoming more and more often. This was my second caesarean section and I wasn't healing well. I was losing the will to live and I knew I had to do something.

That 'something' happened whilst I was tidying the lounge one Friday morning. I found an over-sized gold coin, tucked away in the corner under the stairs. On one side was an image of Jesus' head and on the other side was praying hands, with the words, 'All things are possible, if you only believe,' written around it. I sat looking at the coin, wondering where it had come from and how it had gotten there.

"What do you want me to believe?" I said out loud turning the coin over.

That all things are possible.

"But what do I need to believe is possible? Have you seen my life lately?" I put the coin in my pocket.

"Yes. What are you going to do about it?"

"What can I do about it! In case you haven't noticed, I have no money," I was getting irritated. Did Jesus think I would be here if I had the money to get away? I fought back the tears, I was fed up of crying and I wasn't going to cry anymore.

"Just believe by faith and then nothing is impossible to you."

"I don't even know where to start."

"Remember the house you asked me for?" I stood to my feet, pacing up and down to help jog my memory.

"You don't mean that big one on Colorado Road! That was ages ago, that must be sold by now," I insisted. However it was a light bulb moment that lit a tiny flame of hope inside of me. I didn't act on the thoughts that continually ran through my mind, instead I locked it away safely inside me and carried on reading and praying the way Duncan expected me to. I wasn't allowed to go anywhere by myself and if I did behind his back, it would cause arguments. When there were family gatherings, I played the couples game. We were the perfect example of married life on the outside, and we were often congratulated on our lovely family. I had gotten good at pretending, wearing long sleeves to cover the bruises.

And when it was too apparent that not even foundation could conceal, I would lie and make up stories to concerned friends and to anyone who would ask.

"I hit my face against the edge of the wardrobe," I would say sheepishly, daring not to look them in the eye. And I don't know whether they believed my story or not, but even if they doubted, they did not press any further. I pretended they didn't know, and they pretended they didn't see, either way there was no one to help me. There was no one to confide in, and in the church, you stood by your husband, you never talked bad against him, even when you struggled to take a breath to talk because your ribs were bruised.

Duncan and I took the children to see the horses and have a picnic one weekend and when we returned, I pulled a newspaper from the letterbox as we went into the house. I placed it on the hood of the pushchair as I negotiated the step onto the porch, and then took my sleeping son out and gently laid him in his rocking cradle. Two weeks later I had the sudden urge to find the paper I had put on top of the pushchair. I hurriedly went through the stack of papers in the magazine rack. Something was important about that paper, I just knew it. It was as if my insides were prodding me and I had to find it. Finally, I pulled it out, sat down and began to flick through it, hoping that whatever it was that was so important would reveal itself. A section of the paper fell out onto the lounge floor. I quickly picked it up and placed the newspaper next to me in a crumpled heap. It was the property supplement pages.

"Huh," I said out loud, promptly scanning for something significant. I was about to give up when I noticed a small printed advert at the back left hand corner of the page. I couldn't believe my eyes, my heart started beating in anticipation as I read.

"My house!" I said in amazement. *Could this be the same house I asked Jesus for?* There was no picture, so I couldn't be sure. *Was this the 'possible' He wanted me to believe?* Hope surged through every sinew in my body and my emotions came alive once again - I had to find out. I didn't want to get too excited, after all it may not be the house, but I couldn't stop myself, hope was all I had.

"Thank you Jesus!" I wanted to shout for joy, but Benji was asleep in his rocking cradle next to me. *How was I going to find out without Duncan knowing I'd left the house?* He had a way of questioning Mia about what she did, where she went and who she met, and she was happy to tell him with the innocence and honesty of a typical three year old. I took the coin I found weeks before and held it in my fisted hand.

"I have to find a way!" The words echoed in my head and a determination rose in my heart as I read the words on the coin again, 'All things are possible if you only believe.'

I couldn't deny the spark of hope that was now being fanned into flames with every waking moment. The mortgage payments were beginning to be a strain with just one salary, not to mention the other household bills. As we sat one evening discussing our options, courage appeared to come from deep inside of me and I mentioned the house I saw for sale, explaining that it would be an opportunity to have an extra income.

"I could do childminding and eventually turn it into a nursery," I suggested as he sat looking at the paper, "and I would still be at home looking after our children." Duncan sat silently, his forehead creased and his lips pursed.

"We can't afford a big house like that, it says six bedrooms and three reception rooms," he rose to his feet hitting at the paper, growing agitated as he spoke.

"Can we just phone the agents and go and have a look? If it is suitable to start a nursery, then at least we can work things out from there. The last thing we want to do is lose our home," I said convincingly. "It would be better to sell this house and move to somewhere that has the opportunity to generate income than to stay stuck with all this financial pressure on you." I sat calmly as he paced the floor. "Otherwise I could always go back to work and put the children in a nursery," I stated boldly. He turned sharply and looked at me through narrow eyes.

"No!" His voice echoed with anger, "I told you before and I'm telling you for the last time, you are not leaving my children to go to work." He threw the paper at me and walked up the stairs. I hoped the thought of me going to work would accelerate his thinking. Two days later he told me to phone the estate agent and make an appointment to view the house. I was so happy that as soon as he left for work, I shouted and danced around my house.

As the agent opened the inner front door we were

presented with corridors covered in original coloured floor tiles, with a grand oak staircase that led to the first floor.

"Wow, Duncan, this is so grand." He didn't respond. I had no idea what he was thinking but as we walked around the house, a chill ran down my spine. It was exactly as I dreamt it would be and the excitement within me was growing. It was a large three storey house with an attic and a cellar. The attic had two bedrooms and a wide landing that overlooked the second floor.

All things are possible if you believe.

Could all this be possible? Yes, yes it could be. My heartbeat accelerated with hope as I opened a door to a bathroom, then another to a separate toilet. I tried to contain my excitement as I followed the corridor and found two huge bedrooms and an additional room that could be converted into a kitchen diner. I slid my hands along the polished, dark oak banister, faith adding a spring in my step, as we went down the stairs to three reception rooms. The back room was the largest, with an elegant marble fireplace, and a sleek vintage silver mirror above. Black and white wooden panels framed glass double doors, which opened to a large mature garden, with plum and apple trees. The hedge was made up of blackberry and holly bushes. The garden seemed to stretch beyond our view, and I could imagine Mia and Benji running and playing out there.

The door from the kitchen led outside to a coal shed, toilet and utility area. I stood for a while taking in all the original features of the house, the ceiling coves engraved with roses and the deep skirting boards. It was beautiful.

Do you believe?

My heart answered back, *Jesus I want to believe, but it's not just my decision.* I hurried to join Duncan and the agent as they walked into the front room with its large bay window and yet another marble fire place. The agent led us back to the front of the house through the side gate. It was indeed a grand house, my house.

Our house sold the very day the sale board went up and it wasn't long before we moved into our new home and started the nursery. I was no longer isolated with the staff, parents and children coming and going. The nursery was becoming successful and Duncan was no longer in control of all the finances and he couldn't stop my sisters or friends coming to visit me. He continually told me that the nursery wouldn't work and I should close it down, at times he physically put his point across. His demeaning words were beginning to wear me down, and started to become the words I thought about myself. The stressful atmosphere affected my health and everything I ate burned my stomach which limited my diet. I lost weight rapidly and would pass out without warning. I wanted to die.

It was Saturday morning and I was relieved that I didn't have to go down stairs to work and put on my happy mask. My morning was greeted by a letter from the health centre telling me that my blood test results had arrived and the doctor wanted me to come in to discuss the results. I went to the surgery Monday morning and as I sat waiting to be called, I picked up a magazine and flicked through it in an attempt to stop my mind over-thinking my results, but the magazine had articles about all different kinds of illnesses, some of which matched my symptoms. I put the magazine back on the table and looked at the information posters around the room instead. That didn't help either, if it wasn't about how to recognise heart attacks it was about a stroke, so I just twiddled my thumbs, looked at my feet and eavesdropped on the other patients' conversations. At last my name was called and I made my way to the consulting room.

The doctor was very animated as he greeted me and invited me to sit down with a hand gesture. I smiled and reciprocated his greeting as I sat down. He flicked through my file.

"Umm, aha." He closed the file and looked at me, "Your results were fine Mrs Turner," he reported putting down his pen next to the closed file. My shoulders relaxed as I breathed a sigh of relief. "But something is going on that is causing all these external symptoms," he said rubbing his forehead. "My job as your doctor is to make sure you are fit and healthy and you are obviously not, so there must be something that the blood tests are not telling me. I'm concerned that you are in pain and you have lost a lot of weight, but I don't believe that it is just medical," he said, looking at me, his forehead creased with concern. He sounded like the doctor talking to my mother as I sat listening years before. "Would you like to talk to me about it?" he said cutting into my thoughts, looking straight into my eyes.

I was taken by surprise by his question and

immediately put up my emotional guard. I didn't know what to say. No one had asked me that question before and although I had secretly wished that someone had, I was now lost for words. My emotional guard deserted me as tears filled my eyes and spilled over running down my face and onto my lap. The doctor handed me a box of tissues and I pulled out a few and dried my face looking up at him anxiously.

"Mrs Turner, there has been too many emergency visits to your home and unless you tell me what's happening I can't help you," he coaxed as he patiently waited for me to speak. Between sobs and sniffles I cautiously told him the short version of events at home. Seeing my distress he reached into his desk and took out a small card and handed it to me. "This is the name and address of my solicitor," he said as I took the card. "Go and see him. I'm not saying he has the answers, but he will advise you as to the first step to take."

"I can't afford to go to a solicitor," I replied abruptly.

"Don't worry about that, just tell him I sent you," he reassured me as I rose to my feet.

"Thank you," I put the card in my pocket.

"I want to see you next week. Make an appointment at the desk before you leave. We need to work on fattening you up," he chuckled as I walked to the door.

I left the doctor's office that morning with mixed emotions. I wanted to phone the solicitor's office right away, not that I had any idea of what the procedure would be and then there were the children, and what would my father say? Duncan and my father had built a good relationship, and he wanted him to become a deacon in the church. He was against even the mention of the word divorce! Not that I had made my mind up to get a divorce, but I was under no illusion of the possibility.

Duncan greeted me at the door with a smile.

"What did the doctor say? Did he tell you it's the nursery that's wearing you out and you need to close it down?"

"No."

"What do you mean no?" His smile disappeared as quickly as it came and his eyes narrowed. "I told him last week that you were working too hard and it was making you sick!"

"Why, why would you talk to my doctor about me behind my back?" I stared at him in disbelief! *How far was this man willing to go to control me?* I pushed past him and went upstairs as the realisation of my situation hit me. *I can't do this anymore.*

Finally I made an appointment and went to see the solicitor, who advised that my husband and I attended counselling before any major decision was made. This appeared to make matters worse for me at home and it became an unhealthy environment for the children, so a year later I filed for divorce.

I struggled to go to the garden to meet my friend Jesus. The church made it clear that divorce was a sin, but offered no explanation or advice as to how I could sort out the misery in my life and at home. According to the church I had broken a sacred vow and I thought that Jesus wouldn't want to talk to me again. But how wrong was I.

It was as if He knew when I needed Him most and would come wherever I was. I just had to ask. Whenever we spoke He never once condemned me.

Then one day as I was about to leave the garden, He gently held both my hands in His. Looking directly at me He said,

"Beth, I want you to forgive your husband." The words stung me like an angry bee. I couldn't believe He was asking me to do this!

"Me, forgive my husband after all the awful things he did to me! Is he the victim here?" I snapped pulling my hands away. I couldn't believe what I was hearing!

"It is important Beth. If you don't, it would mess up your life and our relationship." His eyes were dark with sadness as he held my hands once more.

"But Jesus, I lost my home, my business and my dignity, and you want me to forgive him?" I questioned in pleading tones.

"Forgiveness is about your happiness, your freedom," He continued.

"I have to go," I couldn't stand there and listen anymore, it just didn't make sense.

My love and trust in Jesus was shaken as I left the garden that day, and I began to see Him as another dominant male, not as the friend I had come to depend on. So for many years I didn't go to the garden. I wanted nothing more to do with Jesus, church or anyone that spoke about Him.

But His words kept coming poking at me, nudging me, until one day I couldn't take it any longer, so I went to visit the local church. My father had retired and new leaders had taken his place. I didn't know them or recognise many of the people sitting in the congregation, but a few familiar faces greeted me. I'm not sure why I went to this particular church that morning, there were many other churches I could have visited, but for some reason I didn't think Jesus would be there. Nothing much had changed except the decor which was brighter and more modern than before. We sang all the usual familiar songs, the secretary gave the notices, and the offering was collected after a long speech and a prayer that made you feel guilty enough to drop more money in the offering plate. The visiting speaker was eventually introduced and greeted the congregation.

"I came here to preach, however as I sat through the worship I felt God telling me I should tell you my testimony instead, so forgive me if I don't preach you an inspiring sermon, but I must obey my Lord."

Her story was very much like mine and at times I thought she was talking about me. She elaborated with verses from the Bible that sounded very familiar, for the most part about forgiveness and every time she said the word 'forgive' it would stab at my heart. Then I heard her say, "but Jesus told me to forgive my husband if not it would mess up my relationship with Him. I was not happy but I did it anyway, because the relationship I had with Jesus was too precious to lose."

He's here! Jesus was right there asking me yet again to forgive. I had buried the resentment deep inside me for so many years, I didn't know how to let it go. I fought back the tears and tried to control my emotions. *Calm down!* *You are not having a meltdown. Not now!* I scolded myself. My thoughts were interrupted by a gentle touch on my shoulder which suddenly made me look up to a lady's smiling face.

"Could you make your way to the room on the right please? The preacher would like a quick word with you before you leave," she said softly and waited for me to follow her.

I hesitated for a few moments to compose myself then followed. Questions raced through my mind. *Why would she want to speak to me? I don't even know her.* As I entered the room she introduced herself and invited me to sit down.

"So you are the reason I had to change my plans this morning," she said smiling. "He must love you very much," she continued as she took both my hands and held them securely in hers. It felt like an electric surge was coming from her body through her hands and into mine. I started to shake as I fought the tears that welled up in my eyes and trickled down my cheeks. I hadn't cried for a while and had become an expert at burying my emotions and locking away any feelings that made me vulnerable. Even the counsellor the doctor had organised for me to see, gave up after a few sessions. But this time I just couldn't control it. She put her arms around me and tears fell like heavy rain. I cried helplessly, each sobbing breath emptying my heart of all the resentment I had held in for so long. After a while I sat up, she handed me a bunch of tissues, and sat quietly as I dried my eyes and wiped my face in an attempt to look decent. Once I had settled myself she took both my hands into hers, lifted my chin and looked into my eyes.

"Write your husband a letter and let him know you forgive him, ask him to forgive you, not because you have done anything wrong, but because you need freedom from your pain and complete release from your marriage." I looked at her tender eyes filled with tears of concern, I didn't have to explain myself and I didn't have to ask her how she knew. It was obvious - she knew Jesus.

So I wrote the letter and posted it. I decided that would be the last time I was going to church and was determined to avoid contact with anything religious, not to mention I wanted nothing to do with men. Like Jonah I began to run away from my friend.

Chapter 6
Love

Summer had passed and the autumn air was now blowing in. I loved this time of year because the nights were cooler and the mornings smelt fresh, like the air had being cleaned during the night. The old was going out - the brown leaves were being blown away by the wind, to give space for the new to come. Life had definitely changed for me and my children. I no longer had my beautiful house or the nursery and, the pain of losing it gave me a sense of failure. I had lost my dream. With the start of the New Year, I resolved that I had to fight. I sat with my chin cupped in my hands, looking at my reflection in the mirror. I had a deep desire within me to reinvent myself and to ensure that I was going to leave a legacy for my children. I may not have been the Christian everyone wanted me to be, but at that moment, it really didn't matter. I had determination. But what was I going to do with it? How could I change things? I sat on my kitchen table, notepad open and pen twiddling between my fingers.

Write the vision, make it plain.

"Ok Jesus, I can hear you." I rolled my eyes, but really I was glad that I could still hear his voice, despite not having spoken to Him in a while. I closed my eyes, and saw the old house where we used to live when my brother was born.

"Uh," I quickly opened them. There was no way I was going back into my past, not when I had come this far.

"I need a new vision," I stated loudly and closed my eyes again, and this time I could see the dining room of the old house - and her back. I always saw her back and not her face, which was always turned away from me as she worked tirelessly at the sewing machine. This was her livelihood. She seemed to enjoy creating, designing, and sewing unique outfits for women.

As a child, I would stand by the kitchen sink and watch her every move. The way her hands slid across the fabrics with confidence as she draped her designs across the dressmaker's dummy. She never used a pattern, she would listen to what the client wanted and then create the design - and it always worked. I was amazed at how the rough fabric edges were transformed into elegant finished designs.

"Beth, come, come and look at this," she called me one day. I had been watching her for months from afar. This was the first time she had ever let me come near enough to see properly. Nervously, I walked over and stood behind her, peering over her shoulder.

"Beth, come round, you can't see from there." Silently I moved around, and sat on the chair next to her. Her voice was softer than usual, so I looked up in her eyes, not sad, but tired.

"You see this, take the button like this, and line it up with the button hole. Then take the needle and thread and go through like this. Here, you do it now."

"M...me," I stammered.

"You've watched long enough, it's about time you started to help me," she smiled faintly. I carefully took the fabric, and passed it through my fingers. It was beautiful. I couldn't believe she was letting me do this! *Concentrate Beth, you have to get this right,* I told myself.

She stood over me, quietly encouraging me.

"Yes that's right, pull it through, careful now." Her soft voice began to put me at ease. "Good, now do the others for me." I smiled to myself - she trusted me to do this, she even seemed proud of me. She moved back to the sewing machine, rolled the fabric in her fingers and delicately passed it through the machine. It purred gently, as she rhythmically controlled its speed with the pedal. She looked up and motioned with her head for me to carry on.

This was the first of many lessons to come. I excelled at sewing as it came naturally to me. Mum was glad for the help and was very impressed with how quickly I picked things up. She only had to show me once and I could replicate it. I appreciated this new side of her, a softer, kinder, happier side that I had never experienced before. We had something that we both loved that bonded us together. The distant, silent woman I had known, started to become a mother to me.

"That's it," I exclaimed, my past had given me a skill I had overlooked. I looked down at my notepad, tears had stained the page. I knew exactly what I wanted to do. I had a new dream. I began to draw furiously, filling pages and pages with designs, interior layouts and colours. The pages began to come alive. I had to show this to Mum. She would understand it.

The next day I took the children to see her. Full of excitement I sat next to her, showing her design after design of wedding dresses and shop floor plans. I sat back and waited to hear what she would say.

"I like it Beth," she turned to me, "I always wanted to do something like this. You're brave, you've got the courage, you can do it."

My eyes widened. She liked my idea, she really liked it. A smile crept across my face.

"Oh Mum, you don't know how much it means to hear you say that," I threw my arms around her and pulled her tightly to me. I could feel her resistance, this is not something we did, we did not show emotion. Slowly I let her go, things were indeed changing. *I was bold, I could do this - I could do this, right?* I slowly sat back down.

"Mum what if I fail again, you know I've gotten it wrong before?"

"Young Lady, listen to me. Don't let me hear you talk

like that. You have more skill in that little finger of yours, than some of them youngsters out there. You can do this, remember it's Christ who gives you the strength."

I smiled, she believed in me. "Thanks Mum."

That's all I needed to hear. I booked myself onto a short business course, in an attempt to keep me focused and also to get some practical training about starting a business. I sat in the training room, listening to the lecturer, but my thoughts began to wander. *This is brilliant! Am I really going to do this? Start my own business, be a designer?* Before I knew it the class had begun to move into groups, and I had missed the lecturer's instruction.

"Great start Beth," I muttered under my breath.

"Hi Pretty Lady, would you like to join our group?" His alluring accent captivated me. I slowly looked up and our eyes met. His dark skin was smooth and gentle, and his small deep set eyes were quick and mischievous. I was mesmerised. Nodding my head, I slowly regained my voice.

"Yes, thank you."

Those three words were the beginning of a whirlwind romance. His name was Raoul, he was Brazilian, and when he spoke, he aroused in me, feelings that I had never felt for a man before. He was different from the men I had known. He was kind, sensitive, gentle and attentive. He knew just how to treat a woman, like me. I had the flowers, the gifts and unusual surprises. I was treated like a Princess. I had vowed I would never trust another man again - but Raoul was different. He was

Brazilian for goodness sake. He had created in me a desire to open my heart, a desire to be loved and cherished. With Raoul I was a woman, a feminine, strong yet beautiful woman. And I didn't want it to end. This was the sort of relationship I had wanted, but didn't dare dream exist and now, I was living it.

When the business course ended, I decided to work with a childcare agency to gain some extra income whilst I set up the business from home. Then one day, a ray of hope shone into the door of my dream, which would enable me to take the first step on my journey to designing.

"Raoul," I shouted excitedly down the phone, "I have my first order!"

"That's great my Darling. What is it?"

"A wedding dress and five bridesmaid dresses."

"Wow! What a great start. We'll celebrate as soon as I get back."

"Ok. I'm a little nervous though. What if I…"

"Beth, don't! You know how talented you are. You can do this. I can't wait to see your creation," he said confidently, before I had a chance to dwell on the negatives.

"You're right," I sighed, "See you soon."

"Bye my love," he blew a kiss down the phone and he was gone.

I busied myself with sewing and working at the agency. My living room was no longer a place to relax, instead it was a tangled mess of fabric, threads and books. The dining table was no longer a place for food, conversation and laughter. It was now occupied with sewing machines, scissors and pattern pieces. I frowned as I placed my work bag on the chair, scanning the ever increasing clutter. It reminded me of the dining table where Mum and I sat and sewed many years before. The disarray and untidiness caused a few heated arguments between Mum and Dad and now I understood why. I was so fed up with the constant chaos and lack of space. I dreaded to think how the children must have felt. At least Raoul worked away, so he had a break from it all.

The front door opened and I rushed out of the living room to greet him as he came through door.

"Hi," I threw my arms around his neck. He dropped his bag held me close and kissed me.

"I missed you my Princess," he whispered into my ear, holding my waist as he led me into a waltz. I laughed as we turned and swirled into the living room. The limited space brought me back to reality as I knocked my foot on the chair leg.

"Ouch!" I frowned and sat on the chair. He cleared a piece of fabric off another as he sat next to me rubbing my foot. "I need to find somewhere to do the sewing," I said agitated.

"Ok. What's brought this on?"

"This clutter!" I stood to my feet and threw my hands open. He came to where I was standing, mimicking my actions.

"You mean this mess," he wrapped his arms around me holding me tight. "Don't worry about it my darling, we'll look around for a place and I will make it fit for a

Princess," he swung me around playfully.

"Do you mean it?" I questioned, "It only needs to be a space a little bigger than this," I said excitedly as I looked around, pulling away from his embrace.

"Yes," he smiled.

"Ah," I let out a little scream of excitement, "Thank you!" I fell back into his arms, grateful for his love and understanding.

My dream was becoming a reality and it wasn't long before we found a workspace, perfect for the business. I pulled out my notebook of ideas to show Raoul.

"Do you think this would work in this space?"

"Umm," he looked at my drawings, then looked around thoughtfully. "You will need a bigger space for all this, but you can still have some elements of your design layout." Sensing my disappointment, he put his arm around my waist, drawing me close to his side. "Don't worry Beth, it will look just as beautiful, only a little smaller."

"You're right," I sighed deeply, "I can live with that I guess." To get a bigger place would cost more than I could afford right now. But at least this was another step towards my dream, another step which needed to be taken. We worked tirelessly refurbishing the studio in between our day jobs.

"Beth I have something to show you," his eyes were bright and mischievous. I looked at him with suspicion. "Come on," he said taking my hands and leading me out the door and into the car. I sat in silent anticipation, as we drove down the familiar road to the studio.

"Is the studio finished?" I questioned, clasping my hands trying to stop the butterflies fluttering in my stomach. He just smiled and kept his eyes on the road. Raoul was at the studio more than me. I hadn't been for a while, because the customer orders had to be done. No amount of prompting was going to make him give up his secret, and secrets were one of his strong points. I sighed. Raoul was spontaneous which I loved, but at the same time, elusive. His job often took him away from home which was fine at first. But the more I got to know him, the more I realised that I didn't know him at all. His words were careful almost guarded and I was not always in his circle of trust. *Was I one of his secrets?* I shook the thoughts out of my head, I didn't want anything to spoil this moment. We arrived and he opened my car door and held my hand as I stepped out.

"Close your eyes," he said as he playfully covered my eyes and led me through the door. The room smelt of the fresh paint, and the once soundless floor echoed with each step. "Now open them," his voice resounded in the empty room. I stood and stared, then slowly turned around, taking in the amazing sight. The dirty walls were now gleaming white, with a large mirror and wall lights that radiated upwards, giving the smooth walls proportion. The dark, grimy floor was transformed with polished wooden floors. My workspace had wall cupboards and shelves to accommodate all the fabrics and threads I would ever need. At the window were different height podiums, ready for the mannequins that would display the different dress designs. The cutting table and space for my machines made it look professional and ready for business.

"Oh Raoul, this is wonderful!" I flung my arms around his neck and kissed him. He folded his arms around me and held me close. "Thank you," I said looking at him lovingly, he leaned back in and kissed me again, a long lingering kiss.

"It's my pleasure Princess," he danced me along the newly laid floor as he hummed a tune. It was spontaneous moments like these that chipped away at my resistance to love him.

Although our romance was still fresh and exciting, it was often like being on a fast train heading for new adventures. But something was not quite right - the train was slowing down and I had more time to think. The walls of my trust were shaken and the cracks were deep. I questioned myself, often blaming my past for not trusting or believing all that he told me. I gave him the benefit of the doubt, even when some things didn't make sense. He was as charming as ever, but I had to trust my intuition, something was definitely not right. As the train slowed to a halt, I slowly got off. *Did I want to end this relationship?* Standing alone on the empty platform, I rubbed my arms in an attempt to warm them. I sat leaning my head back on a cool wooden bench. Closing my eyes, I thought of all the good times we had and smiled. The memories began to warm me. I remembered the time my son held our hands together.

"Come Mom, I've got something for you," he was excited as he pulled Raoul and me together. "Sit there," he pointed to the sofa. Amused we went along with his plan, curious to see what Benji was up to. Raoul took my hand in his and gently kissed it.

"I love you my Princess," I struggled to respond and was relieved when Benji returned with a reel of thread, his glossy black plaits bouncing as he walked towards us.

"What is that for?" I asked curiously.

"Wait and see!" His eyes were bright with excitement. "Now put your two fingers together," he ordered. Raoul and I did as we were told. Benji wound the thread around first my finger and then Raoul's. "There, you two are married now," he said with a big grin on his face, as he sat and linked his arms in ours. I froze. Marriage was not something I would ever want, not with Raoul, not with anyone. Sheepishly I laughed trying to hide the sinking feeling within me.

"Why thread, Benji?" I asked bringing the focus back to him.

"I couldn't find any rings," he frowned.

"Ah, that's ok. Thank you for our lovely rings," I said hugging him. Raoul tapped my shoulder to get my attention.

"Do you think he knows something that we don't know?" He smiled and winked.

Yes Raoul was kind and thoughtful and I couldn't expect him to be perfect. I sure wasn't. I braced myself as a train of thought sped past me with a strong breeze of guilt that blew into my face. What was I thinking! Benji loved Raoul like he was his own father. In fact Raoul had been there for him, when his own father, had rejected him. How could I do this to him? How could I take away the one person who had become his security, a male figure he could depend on?

The problem was, our relationship had no solid foundation and the only thing that was holding it together now, was a thread of love, which could break at any time. *But, was it my love or his?* I shivered as a cold chill reminded me of the reality that I was alone on this platform. Memories only keep you warm for a while.

"Oh Jesus, what have I done," I said out loud burying my head in my hands. I paced up and down thinking about all the times Jesus came knocking on my door. My heart missed a beat as I winced at the thought. Many times I had left the door closed watching His sad face as He walked away. Jesus wanted me to meet His family and nothing was hidden from me. I had never met Raoul's family and he had never made the effort to introduce me. There were too many secrets and I was beginning to feel insecure. Raoul wasn't a bad person, he loved me, didn't he?

But then there was also this yearning to find Jesus, to go into the garden and talk with Him, to feel His love. Raoul didn't believe in God. He made that quite clear at the beginning of the relationship and to be truthful, that was part of the attraction. I somehow believed that if I was with Raoul, Jesus would stop calling round. But Jesus kept coming, telling me how much He loved me and wanted me back, but I didn't reply and I didn't go to the garden to meet Him.

Come to me Beth.

No I couldn't not after so many years of neglecting to get in touch. I was afraid. I had let Him down. I was living against all the principles of the church. Raoul didn't judge me, he made it easy to be me. But was I being me, by closing myself off from the reality of the garden, the pureness of His love?

Raoul and I had both become quite busy with running a business and working extra hours, so we didn't spend much quality time together, hence the holiday. I sat in the warm hotel room alone, my heart aching for his company. He had gone off by himself again. I knew my love for him was slowly fading, but I didn't want to hurt him. He loved me and was so good to me. His kindness outweighed the things I didn't like. But even if I was mistaken, was the journey back to where I was happy with him, now too far to travel?

I will never leave or abandon you.

This wasn't the time, I didn't want to hear Him now. I walked over and leaned on the balcony looking down at the pool. My heart throbbed watching the other couples, as they laughed and played. Raoul and I didn't seem to have much to talk about lately, and I wasn't sure why he wanted me to come on this holiday with him.

"Beth, be grateful." I warned myself. *I seem to be talking to myself more and more lately.* I thought about my children and how fast they were growing up. My daughter had already moved out, and my son wasn't far behind. He was doing his own thing now and I knew it wasn't long before he would be gone too. I really didn't want to take them through another broken relationship. I wiped a tear of remorse from my eyes, I felt guilty that I had not been a good example to them. *Why don't I have the ability to hold down a good relationship? What's wrong with me?*

"Hi my Darling," Raoul startled me as he came up behind me, holding my waist, he kissed my neck, "Why are you so jumpy?" he swung me around to face him, searching my eyes. I quickly lowered them.

"I didn't hear you come in," I stammered. He lifted my chin and kissed my lips. I didn't respond. He held me close and wrapped his arms around me as we stood in silence. It was unspoken, but maybe he knew too, our hearts were no longer entwined.

It was early evening when he walked out of the door. I wasn't expecting him to leave right away, I felt a little awkward by his eagerness. In a way I was relieved that I didn't have to face him the next morning. I wasn't expecting the mixed emotions I felt inside me. I wanted to cry, but couldn't. *What had I done? Why was his protest not convincing? I bet he just needed the all clear, all this time wanting to go.* I squeezed my hands around my ears in an effort to stop the questions that marched through my head like soldiers going to war. Tears filled my eyes as I glided my hands along the white wooden bed frame, recalling the day I came home to this beautiful bed Raoul had made for my Valentine's present. I recalled the many early morning conversations we would have, that often turned into heated discussions. We had differences which became overwhelmingly apparent especially when I mentioned my friend Jesus. He didn't mind me going to church but couldn't understand this 'God thing,' taking over my life. Church was clear to him, it made sense, but when I tried to explain how real Jesus had become to me, how we had become friends, he became infuriated.

"Why couldn't you just go to church, and not let it brainwash your mind?" he antagonised. I couldn't answer him, he didn't understand. Jesus was too real to me, and too non-existent for him.

And now it was all over. What if he came back? Could I deny my love for him? Would I continue to deny Jesus?

"Beth, let me help you."

"Why! Why would you want to help me?" I retorted angrily.

"Because I love you."

"Do you know how many times I have heard that lately, but it didn't do me any good, did it!" I answered through clenched teeth.

"I am not a man that I should lie."

"You just couldn't leave me alone, could you? Every time I tried to make it work with him, I could hear your voice. You had to come poking at me, messing things up!" My heart ached as I slid to the floor and cried until I couldn't cry anymore - the cost was more than I could bear. Abruptly I sat myself up and dried my tears.

"It was my choice, all of it," I declared out loud. I felt torn. I wanted the garden and Jesus, His love with no secrets. He told me that He would never leave me and He would never stop loving me. And at the same time, I wanted Raoul, a man who loved me in a way that I didn't think was possible. But it was flawed. He didn't love the Jesus I loved. My decision was made. If he didn't understand me, how could he truly love me?

Chapter 7
Forgive

The arrival of spring is a time of new birth, of life. Blossom fills the trees and the earth springs forth sprigs of hope. But for me death filled the air, and with it came the sudden passing of my mother sending my life into a whirlwind. I was at her bedside when she died, but her last breath was so peaceful I had presumed she was asleep. I didn't associate dying with such peace and tranquility. Minutes before, she had shuffled in the bed, to find a comfortable position.

She looked up at me, "Beth are you going to be alright?"

"Mum, I'm fine, you just get some rest." I had watched her settle herself and close her eyes. She had drifted off to sleep. The nurse told me she had gone, but it just didn't register. Disbelieving, I had placed my hand on her heart - it was still warm. Dead people were cold.

"She's gone, Beth. Her heart will be warm for a little while," the nurse said patiently. She hadn't been sick, it was all so sudden. In fact I can't ever remember her going to the doctor or a hospital before. I wasn't prepared for this. I had spoken to Mum about coming home with me at the end of the week. She had smiled and held my hand, as if knowing that she was ready to go home to her Jesus. Well, I wasn't ready, and I had no intention of accepting her death. The nurse urged me to go and call my family. I was numb, motionless. The family came. Numb. We talked, and planned and I nodded and smiled in a foggy haze.

I attended the funeral, I looked after my children, I worked in my business. Daily life went on as normal. I hadn't cried. And then I don't really know what triggered the thought, but I remembered thinking I really needed to visit her. So I went to my father's house and ran up the stairs to her room.

"She's not here!" I shouted. My father came out of his room with a puzzled look on his face.

"Who are you looking for?"

I stood frozen, dumbstruck, and my mind wouldn't come up with any words. Then I heard myself say, "I'm not sure."

"You're going crazy!" he laughed circling his hand by the side of his head, turned and went back into his room.

"You are probably right," I murmured and ran down the stairs.

Shutting the door behind me, I hurried into the car and drove home on auto-pilot. I turned the key in the front door and it was then that the thought jumped out at me, like someone hiding in a bush.

"Ahh!" I screamed out holding my chest. I stumbled to the stairs, my heart thumping in pain, "she's gone. She's dead." It was final. The thought struck me as if I was hearing it for the first time. I crumpled to the floor, screaming in agony. My mother's life was over. I had to find her, to be close to her.

I arrived at the cemetery armed with flowers, and looked out my car window to where we had stood three weeks before at her funeral. Sorrow filled my heart as I remembered the sound of the dirt, loud and definite, bouncing off her coffin shouting to everyone that she had gone. Angrily, I wiped the tears from my eyes. *Why cry now?* I hadn't mourned at the funeral, I hadn't acknowledged her death. An indescribable rage welled up inside of me, like a pouncing tiger on its unsuspecting victim, gripping me firm in its claws. Narrowing my eyes, I stepped out of the car and slammed the door shut. There was her mound covered in mud showing the length of her body, surrounded by dead flowers. The angry tiger was now biting at my throat as I looked closer and read my mother's name and a number at the top.

"She's dead... she's dead!" I wailed. I clasped my hands on the top of my throbbing head, my stomach churned, my legs gave way and I fell to my knees, tears blurring my vision.

"How could you!" I looked up to the sky and screamed. Throwing myself across her mound of mud, a feeling of hate gnawed at me. The angry tiger had now taken down its prey and there was no turning back.

"I hate him! It's his fault, why have you left him here and taken her? Why?" I yelled pounding my fists into the mud. My mother was gone. There was so much I wanted to tell her. I needed her to know that I'd accepted her as my mother and how much I had grown to love her. I wanted to tell her that I forgave her for not sending me back home to my grandmother, and that I forgave her for not protecting me when my father beat me in front of those men. But I couldn't tell her that, because it wasn't true. *I am still angry.* Guilt overwhelmed my entire body. *How could I not forgive her? She's dead!* There was so many unspoken things that had passed between us. When I had arrived at her house bruised and emotionally drained from my marriage, she had offered me no words of encouragement or comfort. Her silence hurt me more than the pain that my body felt. But I needed her now. If only she were here now! I would have told her everything, holding nothing back. The child inside me had so many unanswered questions that she alone could answer, but who was going to answer my questions now? I sobbed, the feeling of hopelessness eroding my insides. I was hollow.

I don't know how long I cried for, or if I had fallen asleep, however something disturbed me, causing me to stir. I pulled myself up and sat on the ground. It was silent, there was no one else around. I reached into my pocket and pulled out a tissue to wipe my face as I staggered to my feet. It was getting late and I needed to leave the cemetery before they locked the gates. Between sobs and silent tears, I removed the dead flowers and replaced them with fresh ones, putting the container with the roses by the cross that marked the place where my mother was buried.

Beth.

I swung around, my heart pounding with fright. A cemetery is not the place to be hearing voices! I wanted to run, but fear paralysed my legs and held me to the spot.

Hate is a very destructive emotion that has the ability to lock you in like a prisoner. You must let it go before it destroys you. If you forgive it will have no hold on you.

Relief spread through my body like an anaesthetic as I recognised the familiar voice.

"You again!" I shouted fisting my hands and stomping my feet. "You are always telling me to forgive. You are always telling me to do things I don't want to do," I retorted as I got into the car and drove off like a mad woman. "Why didn't you come when I needed you? Why have you taken my Mum before I had a chance to get some answers! Why?" I shouted thumping the steering wheel. I was out of breath now, a tiredness seemed to come over me.

"I didn't tell her I forgave her Jesus. I didn't expect her to die so soon!" I softened as my words seeped into my heart, cutting it wide open. My hands trembled as I fought to keep control of the car. "She died so soon." Swerving suddenly, I pulled up at the side of the road, I cried like a dam had burst open and I couldn't stop it.

I couldn't go home, I needed some time to calm down and give my puffy eyes a chance to return to some normality. I drove to Rhys Hill and parked the car. I scanned the other cars parked a few feet away on the left and right of me. The couples looked happy as they held each other, some talking, others laughing. It was so peaceful sitting there high above the city. The buildings down below looked tiny with all the different coloured lights. I sat in the dark silence and gazed up at the stars.

"Jesus, I am really sorry for shouting at you and blaming you for my Mum's death. I know that she's with you and at peace, and I know you would never do anything to hurt her or me, but my life is in such a muddle, I don't know which way to turn. Help me please!"

Don't be afraid, I am right here with you. I have never left you and I will help you.

"Thank you," I dried my tears as a wave of peace washed over my broken heart.

⤳⟡⤶

Later that year, my daughter, Mia invited me to watch her dance at a special event held at the church she attended. I was a little apprehensive at first as church and I just didn't agree, but walking into the atmosphere of the people singing, felt like I had stepped into fresh clean air. Mia danced to a song 'Alabaster Box [2]', she was so

---

[2]'Alabaster Box' CeCe Winans (1999)

graceful as she danced a blend of ballet, jazz and mime. The song told the story of a woman's desperate need to get to Jesus. She walked through a room of men's disapproving grunts, angry stares and accusing whispers to where Jesus was sitting. Bowing low she washed his feet with her tears, dried it with her hair and anointed it with very expensive oil. It was as though the dance was expressing everything I was feeling.

I closed my eyes, absorbed in the mesmeric atmosphere. Suddenly the church seemed empty, like I was the only person there. The room was filled with a bright light and I could feel the presence of Jesus all around me. Then He was there, right in front of me. Tears were streaming down my face as the words of the song became a reality to me and I bowed. I looked at His dusty feet and searched for water to wash them, but there was none, so I washed them with the tears that fell from my eyes, as I asked for forgiveness. He leaned down, took my hand as my tears dripped onto His. I looked up to meet His eyes, filled with compassion and love.

"Forgive," he simply said. I knew what He wanted, but the pain inside wouldn't let me. I bowed my head and started to pull my hands back towards me, my own will fighting against His. His hand cupped my face, and I looked back into His eyes, and I knew with His help I could do this, I could release the anger, the pain and forgive.

"I cherish every tear that falls from your eyes Beth, and I'm touched by every situation in your life whether good or bad."

I closed my eyes, the feeling of peace filling the void within my heart as though this was the first time I had ever felt true love. My hands spread outwards and I bowed face down, a new heavenly language filled my mouth. I was overwhelmed by His beauty, by His love, and I couldn't speak in words to express it. I had to worship Him. When I opened my eyes, the song had ended, I had not been alone, the church was full of people. A lady helped me to my feet and trembling, I sat down on my chair.

Going to church ignited my need to meet with Jesus again. Laying in the darkness of my room, the compulsion became urgent. I went into the garden to the place we used to meet, but He wasn't there. I ran through the garden and saw a dusty road ahead which I had never seen before. I frantically ran up the road, searching.

"Jesus, where are you?" I heard voices in the distance and as I got closer, I could hear a boisterous crowd of people causing a commotion. I pushed through the crowd and saw soldiers standing linked arm in arm holding back the angry mob as they shouted,

"Crucify Him!"

I heard the whip go up as it whistled in the air and came down on the body lying across a wooden plank. I looked through the gap of the soldiers' arms and couldn't believe what I was seeing. It was Jesus, but why? Why would they do that to Him? Tears filled my eyes. Desperately I threw my head from side to side in an effort to find an opening to run to Him.

"No, no stop it, stop you're killing Him!" I shouted as

I broke free and ran towards Him.

"Get back you sprat!" the soldier growled as they both grabbed hold of my arms and dragged me away, throwing me like a rag doll back into the crowd. My arm throbbed with pain from the soldiers' grip as I landed with a thud on the ground. Unaware of my own discomfort, I screamed in pain with every whistle of the whip as it came down on Jesus. The memory of my father's belt coming down on me flashed before my eyes as I screamed out. I picked up my aching body from the ground to avoid being trampled on, as the crowd pressed forward. I weaved my way through them as the soldiers started nailing Him to a cross. With every ounce of strength I had left, I pushed my way past the guards like an angry bull and charged towards the soldiers, hammering them with my fists as they pulled the cross up to stand.

"No, no! How could you do this to Him again!" my throat burning as I shouted, my heart breaking with every thud, eyes blinded by tears. I had to stop them! One of the soldiers knocked me to the ground and everything went dark.

I don't know how long I was out for, but when I came round, everything was quiet except for the raging pain in my head. Then my eyes came into focus and there was Jesus hanging on the cross a few feet away from me, blood dripping from His hands and feet, caused by the nails that held Him there, and as I looked up, my swollen eyes met His.

"Why?" I whispered through my bloody, throbbing

lips.

"Because I want you to be free from your guilt and shame, from your pain and rejection, but most of all, because I love you and now sin will have no hold on you," He whispered back.

"I'm so sorry I ran away from you," my voice faint, my speech slow, pausing at every word as the pain ripped through my head. He looked at me with such tender eyes and, I knew at that moment I was forgiven. "How can you forgive me so easily, when all the wrong I did put you there?"

"It was not easy, Beth, but I loved you more than the pain. Each person that comes to me is forgiven from all the wrong things they have done, no matter how bad they are. Everyone that has hurt you is human, and gets things wrong."

"Yes but what they did to me has affected my whole life. Imagine, my life could be so different, I wouldn't be such a mess!"

"Beloved, you have the power within you to change your life. Forgiveness sets you free from the power the pain held over you. They are human Beth, just like you."

I closed my eyes, the pain in my head was so intense and everything went dark again. I felt myself ascending upwards, all the way through the cold darkness towards a glowing light. The nearer I got to the light, the brighter it shone and the warmer my body became. And there stood Jesus radiating brilliant light, as He stood with His arms open wide. He embraced me in welcome, holding me close as I rested my head on His chest.

I took His hands and looked at the scars from the nails.

"That was awful Jesus, I'm so relieved you're not on that horrid cross anymore. How could people do that to you? They are monsters!"

"No Beth, they are human, and I loved them. I died once on that cross for each and every one of them, so that they could always come to me, forgiven and free. All they have to do is believe in me."

I didn't understand why He wasn't angry. I thought about all the wrong that had been done to me. Jesus forgave the whole world, endured all that pain and He didn't do anything wrong! I was nowhere near perfect and I was struggling to forgive.

"Beth," He held my hands and looked me in my eyes, His eyes sparkling like the stars, "Your children need you, it is time for you to go," He said tenderly, "but before you leave, there is something I need you to do." I looked at Him curious to know what He could possibly want from me. He gently squeezed my hands as He continued, "You must go and take back your keys of forgiveness. It will enable you to unlock your ability to forgive and help you to move forward." I was a little taken aback at His request.

"Where do I find these keys?" I asked puzzled.

"Don't concern yourself, I will send my angel with you and He will show you," He said as He waved His hand summoning an angel.

I turned to see a figure of a man standing behind me. He was as bright as light, but had no wings.

"Where are his wings!?" I asked in astonishment, my

mouth dropped open in awe and wonder.

"He doesn't need wings," Jesus chuckled, placing my hand in the hand of the angel. "Take care of her, she's precious," He said softly.

The angel held my hands and I found myself going down. It was getting colder and darker with every falling moment, when suddenly the angel blew a trumpet. The light of the angel radiated and the darkness started to clear into a grey mist. When the mist cleared, I saw large black gates opening to awful screams of hate, low-pitched growls of anger and the groaning's of resentment. The light of the angel unveiled the most indescribable scenes. I covered my eyes from the horror that unfolded and hesitated. The angel held my hand and led me into the dreadful place. The smell of bitterness made me heave and I tried to control the churning in my stomach.

"Come," he commanded, "We do not have much time," he said with urgency. I walked quickly, trying to keep pace with the angel, my mind questioning why Jesus would send me to such a terrible place. *Is this where unforgiveness would live?* The angel suddenly stopped and released me from his grip.

"The next few steps you must take without me. I cannot go any further."

I stood shivering with fear and as I looked ahead, I realised we had come to a dead end. The only light in the place was coming from the angel who stood watching me. His light revealed a massive wall covered in keys of all shapes and sizes. Some hung on their own while others were in bunches. As I moved closer, I looked along the wall and saw familiar names and reached for the keys.

"No! You must only take the one with your name on it," the angel said with irritation.

"Why?" I questioned.

"It is not your responsibility," he answered promptly. "Now hurry!"

"Ok, ok!" I responded and quickly took the keys with my name off the hook. I hurried back to where the angel was waiting. He took my hand and we walked hastily along the corridors to the gate which was about to close. As we ran out, it shut with a loud bang and the angel pulled me up and up again towards the bright light. I found myself back in my room, sitting up on my bed gasping for breath, my arms held tight across my chest trying to ease the pain that threatened to stop me breathing for good.

I heard Mia's voice calling.

"Mom?" I could hear her panicked breathing as she ran up the stairs and burst into my room. "Are you ok?" she asked dropping herself onto my bed, her forehead wrinkled and her eyes large with concern.

"It's just a throbbing headache and some chest pains," I answered taking a breath between each word. "I was just about to phone for an ambulance," I said as she looked at me with enquiring eyes.

"I was at college and had this urgent need to get home. It felt like your life depended on it," she explained as she dialled the emergency number.

That night as I lay in bed, I wrote in my diary, recording all that had taken place. I had the keys to forgiving others and I had a choice to use them or not. I held those people in my heart in that nasty horrible place, I couldn't do that anymore. I had to be free. I had to use the key and free myself and all those that had hurt me.

Chapter 8
Reign

The sun shone brightly into my room through a peep in my curtains, waking me up to a feeling of excitement in the air. I sat up in my bed, a smile plastered across my face. I felt light, like I could float up, just like a feather. I danced my hands up in the air. Throwing back the covers, I bounced out of bed and waltzed around the room.

"Ah," I sighed, my body relaxed at ease. I danced over to the window and swept open the curtains. Outside seemed to reflect how I felt inside. It was a lovely day, sun shining and blue skies. It was Sunday and I was going to church with Mia. The sinking feeling I usually got when I thought of church didn't dissuade me from getting myself ready.

"Not today," I said out loud, "Nothing is taking away my happiness today." I smiled as I did up my black jacket button and eyed myself in the mirror.

"Huh," I said to my reflection, "you're looking good today. Not carrying around anymore of that heavy baggage." It was true, since I had chosen to forgive, and let go of my past, I felt lighter. It was as if I had spent years carrying around everything that had ever happened to me. But today, I was different.

"Welcome to the new me," I beamed at myself throwing my hands up with confidence.

Mia popped her head around the corner. "You're looking happy Mom," she frowned slightly, "are you alright?" I shot her a playful look that told her I was not going to be fazed today.

"I'm playing Mom, you ready? We'd better get going."

I followed her out of the room, filled with a determination that today was a new day, and it would stand to attention and welcome the new me.

As I neared the doors of the church, my confidence started to wane. Sure, I had been here before, and I knew what to expect, but that didn't stop my uncertainty of being at church. Suddenly I was unsure if I really was, the new me. I thought back to how I had sat on my bed full of determination armed with notebook and pen. I wrote every name of every person I could think of that I knew I needed to forgive. I wanted to get this right and a thorough list would ensure I had really forgiven. I may have forgiven everyone that hurt me but I sure hadn't forgotten, and neither had the fear that was rising up within me.

"Go on Mom, go in." Mia pushed me gently through

the doors.

"Hello. Lovely to see you," a smiling lady greeted us. I eyed her slightly and then smiled. *It's going to be ok,* the new me told myself as Mia and I walked down the aisle.

"Would you like to come this way and I will help you to your seats?" another lady said as we followed her to be seated.

The music started, and I felt a little self-conscious. Brushing the sides of my jacket down, I stood and looked around seeing a few familiar faces. There were people young and old singing with their hands lifted in worship, others were kneeling. Mothers sat with their children on their laps, while other children sat swinging their little legs or playing with toys on a chair next to them. There were no hymn books and pews with kneeling pads, instead I read the song words from a large screen at the front of the church. I was relieved it was there because I did not know all those modern songs. The podium was more or less the same as most churches, but there was no choir, instead there was a praise and worship group of around six people. They led the congregation, with musicians on the drums, a keyboard and electric guitars. A few people were seated on the balcony as all the seats in the main auditorium were taken. It wasn't a complicated building, in fact it was simply decorated with white walls and with a couple of picture frames with Bible verses in them. The dark oak balcony gave the space some dimension and depth to an otherwise blank canvas.

I took a deep breath. This was the place I needed to be

right now, around people who knew Jesus. But still I shuffled in my chair, as the singing ended, uncertain about whether I would be accepted here. The preacher stood to speak and I was focused on what he had to say.

"If I was to give this message a title," he said, "I would call it, 'You shall not die but live," he continued in an authoritative voice. "You will live to declare the glory of God!" I'm sure he said other things as well, because he spoke for about an hour, but I didn't hear it. The crowd of people began to clap and shout "Hallelujah!" As he continued to speak, it felt like he wrote the words just for me. He pointed into the crowd.

"Whoever you are, Jesus wants you to know that everything will be ok," his voice got louder. "You will not die but live to declare the Glory of God!" he exclaimed. The music started to play while some people went to kneel at the front, the crowd rose to their feet clapping and singing. The atmosphere was exhilarating, as the people worshipped. This was very different from church as I knew it.

I sat back in my seat and pondered the words. *Yes I will live,* I declared boldly to myself. My morning confidence began to return to me and I felt alive again. I was not going to let my fear of church rob me of my happiness. No I was going to live, and I was not going to deny Jesus the place of living right there with me.

When I got home I went straight into the garden to find Jesus. I didn't recognise the wooden door that stood in place of the gate I often opened. I pushed the door but it didn't open. My curiosity got the better of me and I pushed again. I noticed there was a keyhole, so there must be a key, I thought. I felt around the door and there at the top was a small golden key hanging on the doorpost. I unhooked it and looked at it in amazement. The key was engraved in the form of a dainty rose, with a butterfly resting on it. Carefully I laid it in the palm of my hand examining the letters that made up the tip of the key - Faith. I had never seen anything like it before.

"How unusual!" I said out loud. I carefully pushed the word Faith into the lock. "Yes," I exclaimed it fitted perfectly. I slowly turned the key and took a deep breath, in an attempt to slow the rapid beat of my chest as I pushed the door open. I cautiously stepped into a room and took the key out of the keyhole holding it securely in my hand. I had walked into a beautiful pure white room. There was a stage at the front, draped with the finest green silk curtains that fell from the ceiling to the floor, tied back with a gold cord. The white marble floor twinkled with light, like someone had spilled stars all over it. Facing the stage was a beautiful golden throne decorated with sparkling diamonds, rubies and emeralds making it look almost theatrical. The seat was covered in the most luxurious red velvet fabric I had ever seen. The throne stood majestically on a red heart shaped marble podium that matched the seat of the throne. On the side of the throne was a small table made from pure gold, with a crown that perfectly matched the throne, glistening in the light, and a golden sceptre carefully placed next to it. The arm of the throne was draped with a robe made of purple velvet, lined in dazzling gold satin. I couldn't believe my eyes, my heart thumped in expectancy. *Who does all this belong to? And where is the garden?* At the back of the room I noticed a large white door. If it had not been for the shiny gold door knob, I would have missed it. I quickly walked through the room and opened the door, and to my surprise, I found myself in the garden. Jesus was seated on the bench and as I approached, He stood and greeted me, like He was expecting me.

"I've found a door to a room, that leads to the garden come and see!" I said excitedly, pulling Him in my eagerness and leading Him to the door.

"I know," He said gently as He turned and took both my hands in His, which He had a habit of doing. "Beth, this is the door to your heart. I have been waiting for you to invite me in, not just as a friend, but as your Lord and King. Things will change, and we won't only be meeting in the garden where you can run in and out of the relationship as you please. This will mean commitment."

"Commitment! But I gave you my life Jesus!" I declared boldly.

"Yes you did, but I also want to reside in your heart as well as your life."

I looked into His eyes so tender and kind and I knew He would never abuse His position as Lord and King of my life. I had given my heart to others who used and abused me. But Jesus was different, I was sure that He loved me and whatever plans He had for me were good, not to hurt me, but to give me a future I could look forward to.

"I want you to be my Lord and King of my heart and

my life," I said softly, as I pushed the door wide open and invited Him in.

When He entered, the room glowed with His presence. My hands began to tremble and my body quivered as I held His hand in mine. I led Him to the throne, placed the robe around His shoulders, securing it by the gold clasp that extended from the collar. He sat down, then I placed the golden sceptre in His hand and reached to position the crown on His head. As I did this, the precious key that I had been holding onto fell from my hands. I quickly looked up at Jesus expecting him to be upset. *Uh why didn't I just put it back where I found it,* I scolded myself. I quickly picked it up and handed it to Him feeling a little awkward, like a child caught with her hand in the cookie jar. He smiled as He reached under His robe and took out a small wooden box. He opened it and slowly placed the key in it then took my hand and rested it in my palm.

"Don't let anything or anyone take this from you, without it you cannot come to me," He closed my fingers around the little box. "You see the word faith," I looked down at the key and traced the letters with my finger, "it is important. By having faith in me you will be able to accomplish extraordinary things."

I knelt in reverence, slowly bowing before Him and worshipped Him in a heavenly language which I could not interpret, but He always appeared to understand. I left the throne room of my heart and found myself in my bedroom, bowed to the floor worshipping. My life changed from that day on and was never to be the same again.

I turned the key in the studio door, switched on the lights and walked through to the sewing room. Putting my bags down, I stretched over to the stereo and switched it on. Soft music filled the room with a serene atmosphere as I went to make myself a cup of tea. Holding my cup with both hands, I walked around the studio sipping it. Leaning against the sewing room partition wall, my eyes fell on the small white display cabinets that stood in each corner of the room. Each one was finished with glass shelves that gave transparency to the up lights which shone on the tiaras and jewellery, making them sparkle like diamonds in the sun. They were exquisite. Around the room were mannequins dressed in different wedding gowns, bridesmaids' dresses and children's outfits placed strategically with matching bags, veils and shoes. *I made all of this,* I beamed, the feeling of accomplishment sweeping over me. I walked over to the bouquet of silk flowers, and fingered the petals. They were full of colour, lifting the ambience of room.

Raoul was a brilliant interior designer, I thought to myself, a sinking feeling filling my insides. I missed him - that much was obvious.

"But you've made the right decision," I reassured myself wrapping my arms around my waist. Life was different without him, but the frosty loneliness I had felt when we first separated, was beginning to thaw. The studio always brought back fond memories of Raoul, as we worked tirelessly to meet the studio opening deadline. Sometimes the memories overwhelmed me, when I stood looking around at what he had created.

"No," I said a little too loud, "this is my studio." As hard as we had worked, Jesus had made sure everything I needed had been in place. He had given me the vision, and he had ensured that Raoul was there to help me bring it to pass. I was not going to sit and reminisce, I was going to continue with the vision of the studio.

With a renewed determination I walked back into my sewing room, placed my cup down and picked up the wedding gown I was working on. I loved working on the dresses, creativity flowed out of me with ease. A sudden pain struck me, and I breathed out slowly. Mum had died before she was able to see our dream of the studio become a reality. Sometimes I'd be handling a piece of fabric, and the way it draped around my fingers brought back memories of her shaping her designs. The sounds of the machine often took me right back to my childhood home - me standing watching, with her back to me. I could smile now, because she had drawn me in. I had begun her dream, and I would make this work. Not for her, but for me.

Still smiling I walked over to the stereo and turned up the song that was playing. The song filled the room, an enchanting sound vibrating through the speakers as voices sang, 'Healing water flow over my soul[3]. I looked over at the stereo, the sound seemed to encircle me, and I began to quiver. Their melodious voices lifted the sound bouncing it onto the ceiling, splitting it open to reveal the sky. I looked up, mouth ajar, to see a cloud burst as a voice rang out sweetly, 'Let it rain, let it rain[3]. The rain

---

[3] 'It's Raining' Israel and New Breed (2005)

fell heavier and heavier, each drop falling on my body drenching me from head to toe. As I looked up, it began to wash my face, pure clean rain falling delicately onto my skin. I opened my arms out wide allowing the rain to saturate my body and began to speak in the heavenly language that expressed my adoration and worship, reaching the heart of Jesus.

As the song reached an end, trembling I looked back up at the ceiling and staggered to my feet. The ceiling was in-tact, not split open as it had been moments before. I brushed my arms, to find that I was dry and so was the floor.

"Wow," I said amazed, "That was new, Jesus." I smiled, and spun around. A newfound strength seemed to fill me.

The studio became a haven of peace, calm in the midst of wedding turmoil. I could see myself reflected in the lives of many of the brides, and they would ask me, and confidently I would tell my story: Of men, of love, of choices. And against my better judgement, well against my accountant's advice, I would be a listening ear for their stories and sometimes a shoulder to cry on. Many told stories of rejection, low self-esteem and a lack of confidence and I would more often than not, offer to pray with them.

Could it be that I was spending more time ministering to brides than making dresses for them? I had a newfound passion for women that had been in pain just like me. Some felt trapped, they didn't want to disappoint their families or their friends. And my story seemed to be hope for them, that even when starting again, they too could find strength. A few brides did not go through with their weddings, and my business accounts suffered for these. But for the majority of brides, I designed couture dresses, always making sure it fitted them perfectly whatever their shape or size. Seeing them happy, fulfilled in love, brought hope to me - that one day that would be my story.

Chapter 9

Fear

I breathed a sigh of relief as the last bride left at the end of the day. I turned around and leaned heavily on the closed studio door. It had been a long busy day. I slipped out of my shoes and walked barefoot over to the sewing room.

"Uh what a mess." The silver thread I had been using had chosen to weave itself into the carpet, and the scraps of fabric were everywhere. I slumped onto my swinging chair. I loved the studio. It was my dream, my pride and joy, but it was at times like these that I sometimes wondered if it was profitable. I had never started it to be a money-making machine, but the long hours, and the meticulous handwork, made some of the dresses, more beauty than profit. I was also still working at the children's home part-time to supplement my income, and the combination of the two was starting to take its toll on me.

A loud ring disturbed my tired thoughts. Using my feet I shuffled myself over to the telephone, still on the chair. *Yes it would be quicker to walk,* I thought to myself, but my feet needed a rest. Judith was on the other end of the phone, her voice quick and full of concern.

"Slow down, Judith, I have no idea what you've just said." Judith took a deep breath and explained that my father had been taken into hospital again. I sighed deeply. I was too tired for this today. I had genuinely lost count of the amount of hospital admissions he had had over the last few months.

"Yes, I hear you, no I understand. Ok, it's serious, right. Yes, yes I'm on my way," I responded trying to mask the reluctance in my voice. I had been on my feet all day and I had not seen my children yet, now to spend an evening at the hospital with my father.

"Great," I said out loud, knowing full well I was not being fair.

Slowly, I got up from my chair and grabbed my bag. "This mess will just have to greet me tomorrow."

I got into the car and as I drove, I contemplated what I was going to encounter at the hospital. "I hope this isn't one of his attention-seeking moments," I said out loud.

I arrived at the hospital and was greeted by Judith.

"What took you so long?" her face was creased with concern.

"Sorry, I've just come from work, it's been that kind of a day," I sighed trying to keep my patience. "What's the doctor saying?" I asked coolly.

"I don't know, I was waiting for you to come."

"Ah maybe he is grieving or lonely," I said as we hurried down the corridor towards the receptionist. "This is the third time in a month an ambulance has been called," I said trying to keep pace with her.

"This time it's chest pains," she sighed anxiously.

"But this only seems to happen when he is alone, although he has so many visitors throughout the day. Doesn't that seem odd to you?" I added.

"Let the doctor give us the diagnosis, Beth!" she was getting agitated by my apparent lack of concern.

We sat in the room as the doctor spoke to my father. He looked anxious as the doctor suggested someone from his family looked after him on a more permanent basis. The alternative was him going into a residential home, which appeared to scare him even more.

"It would only be short-term, until a care plan could be put in place for you," the doctor assured him. "At least you would be able to live independently at home," he said as he left the room.

"I don't want to go into one of those residential homes, Beth. I would die if I have to," my father pleaded with me. He wanted me to move into the house with him.

His pleading took me by surprise and made me feel uneasy, and all of a sudden, I wanted to reach out to him – to protect him. This feeling was new to me, but I was not used to the vulnerability and weakness he was displaying. This person lying there was not the father I knew. Even though we didn't often agree, I'd always secretly admired him for his emotional strength, values and beliefs. It seemed as though he had a fear of death, which took me by surprise. He didn't want to go into the residential home, because he felt he would die. I wasn't sure if he was just being dramatic but dying was a bit extreme. I had heard him say boldly many times,

"Do not be afraid of death, if you love the Lord, you will live with Him forever," holding onto the podium, bouncing on his toes in excitement. "Death is only a door to a better life where there will be no more sickness or pain, we will never again have to mourn our loved ones," throwing his hands up in the air as the congregation clapped their hands and said, "Amen" in agreement. This fear of dying wasn't exclusive to my father by any means, but it puzzled me, because I wasn't expecting it from him. *Does God cease to be God when we retire, grow old or sick, and need Him most?* My mother's passing was so calm and peaceful. Why was my father so afraid to go to the very One he spoke about and referred to as his 'Heavenly Father?' This really baffled me. Maybe Jesus' Father wasn't as wonderful as He had made out…

"Okay! I will stay at the house, only until you are back on your feet," I said to calm him.

"Go and find the doctor and tell him," he urged, "then they can discharge me right away," he gestured, showing me out of the room. His countenance changed from a frail, worried old man to a bright eyed, strong human being, ready to get dressed and walk out of the hospital.

"What a mighty quick recovery!" I chuckled, nudging Judith in the ribs.

"He's just like a naughty child who has just got his

own way," she said laughing.

Was I really going to do this? I said to myself shaking my head in defiance. I had no choice, he needed someone. *Uh,* he needed me. *How would this work?* The whole idea seemed ridiculous. *I would have to give up my home, I'd have to uproot my son. No, this is truly crazy. I'd be returning to my childhood home, I would be choosing to live with my father!* I saw the doctor I needed to speak to and slowed my pace.

"Oh I would want my children to do the same for me," I reasoned and headed in the doctor's direction.

Everything was organised and I was in my father's house in record time. My three bedroom house was compacted into one bedroom at my father's. Holding a box, I pushed open my bedroom door. This is where I was to live, for the foreseeable future. I was now a child again, living in my father's house. I dropped the box on the floor and sat down heavily on my bed. My room was now decorated in pure white, with white laminated floors. I had all the old wardrobes and chest of drawers taken out and replaced with my own. I tried my best to remove anything of the past. I cleaned the house from top to bottom and although I couldn't change the decor anywhere else, at least I had my room to escape to if things got too difficult.

It wasn't long before my father started treating me with contempt and the demons of my past persistently tormented me. Nothing I did pleased him, he wouldn't even eat the food I cooked, instead he ordered food and had it delivered.

"Don't forget to get rid of all that fabric your mother left in the back room." I didn't reply. "Did you hear what I said?" he growled.

"I heard you," I said coolly, glaring at him. The atmosphere was edgy and tense. This was not the time to be getting into an argument.

"If you have something to say, you had better say it," he retorted.

"I don't think you are ready for any home truths," I bit back. His eyes flashed with anger as he looked at me. He didn't reply, instead he turned and walked down the stairs.

"Beth you've done it again!" I scolded myself. I threw myself across the bed and wondered if we would ever form a truce. *What was it about me that he disliked so much?* He appeared to get on with everybody else and I'd seen a humorous side to him especially when he entertained his visitors. I often heard their loud laughter from some joke or funny story he would tell. Then there were the few times he would tease Mum making some comical comment around the dinner table. She would laugh and push him playfully. He was loved and respected wherever he went and he had received so much adulation from the community.

What about me, why couldn't we have such a positive relationship? My father and I didn't have a relationship, mainly because we didn't think alike when it came to church and religion. This was strange because he had always been a trailblazer for the Christian faith. He broke down religious barriers, and brought communities together that would never have mixed. Maybe he struggled with me, because we were so much alike. I laughed, *Me, like my father, no chance!* It all made me think about Jesus, meeting His Father. This worried me. *What if His Father treated me like my father did, punish me every time I did something wrong?* I just couldn't be good enough for Father, I messed up every day no matter how hard I tried to do what was right. He was holy. Having a relationship with Him was out of the question.

I entered the throne room and sat down on a step leading up to the throne. Jesus came and sat next to me. I didn't have to explain, He looked at me with eyes that said He already knew how I was feeling.

"Beth, it's not how good you are, or about how often you go to church, read the Bible, fast or pray, or even how brilliantly you preach. Although these things are important, you must be careful that it doesn't just become a religious act. If you keep trying to impress Father you will struggle, He only responds to your faith."

"Oh Jesus, this is so hard to understand, because this sure feels like I'm being punished right now, being back here living with my father."

"That's why you must believe by faith. There's no reason for Father to punish you, He loves you and wants a real relationship with you."

"I will have to trust you on this Jesus," I sighed as I left the throne room. I sat up and continued filling the last bag of odds and ends, to drop off at the charity shop. The fabrics and the sewing machine would have to be taken to my studio later.

The doorbell rang and I hurried downstairs to open it. The social workers from the hospital had arrived. I introduced myself and showed them into the living room where my father was waiting.

"You can leave us now Beth" he said.

"It's ok Mr Turner, we need Beth to help us make the best decisions for your care," the social worker replied.

"No, it's ok. I'm quite capable of doing that for myself," he insisted. I excused myself from the room in an effort to conceal my embarrassment, after all it was his choice.

I left the house and walked to the park I needed some air. Wiping the tears of anger from my eyes, I ran into the throne room of my heart and screamed.

"Why me Jesus, why me!?" I dropped to my knees, buried my head in my hands and cried. "You know how much he hates me! Why did he ask me to move to the house? I thought you said it was ok to go and help him! How could I have been so wrong?" He didn't interrupt me as I sobbed. When I was all cried out, He reached out and helped me to my feet.

"Jesus I really thought there was a chance to build some bridges," His eyes were saddened by my pain.

"Be strong and brave my love."

"I don't feel strong right now. I'm so hurt and angry, I just want to run away!"

"Beth, this battle isn't yours, it is mine," Jesus was calm as he held me close. An hour had passed and I needed to get home, so I left the throne room and hurried back to the house.

I got there just as the social workers were leaving.

"Hi again Beth," one of the ladies greeted me, "everything is set up for your father. We will send you a copy of the care plan as you are his main carer," she said, waved and left.

My father looked at me, narrowed his eyes and huffed all the way up the stairs to his room. I took a deep breath.

"Jesus it's a good thing this battle is yours and not mine!" I wanted to go home, but I had no home to go to. I remembered Becca telling me not to get rid of my house and I wished I had listened.

I couldn't comprehend the intense feeling of evil that repeatedly plagued me. The nights brought terrifying nightmares, which woke me out of my sleep screaming in fear. Some nights I didn't even bother to go to sleep. On one such night in my desperation, I decided to read my Bible to see if there was anything to help me understand. Turning the pages, I walked into where David was pouring out his heart to God about the things Saul had done to him. He had done nothing to warrant the hatred of Saul, in fact he helped him win the fight against the country's enemies. David was bent over just like I often was, holding his stomach and sobbing uncontrollably asking God to help him. After a while David stood and lifted his hands towards heaven and started praising God for protecting him. David was only a boy when he went to live in the palace with King Saul. He behaved well and did everything to please Saul, but Saul despised him. I identified with David as I remembered how I had tried everything to please my father, but he never once said well done or thank you. *How strange, David never once dishonoured Saul.* He still respected him as his king. I stood looking at David as he praised God, and wondered how he found it within himself to go from crying his heart out, to giving thanks.

I walked away from David into the throne room of my heart to talk to Jesus. I knelt by His feet and told him about the fears of being back in my father's house and the nightmares that woke me up every night.

"I know you told me to be brave, but I really can't take this anymore," I said throwing my hands up in the air.

"Don't be afraid Beth. I will never leave you or let anything harm you." He said softly looking into my eyes. "Like David you will have to trust me with your life. You must have faith even when things get dark and difficult." A wave of peace washed over me, it felt like something heavy had been lifted off me. "Now lie down and sleep in the comfort of my peace and safety."

"Thank you," I said as I rose to my feet. I danced as I worshipped Him, my heart at peace again. Jesus laughed and clapped like a proud parent, with every spin and twirl I did. Now I understood how David could go from tears to worship.

"Beth, remember you must honour your father regardless of his behaviour," He chided.

"I'm trying Jesus," I sighed.

I left the throne room of my heart and walked into the warm glow of the sun shining through my bedroom window. It was morning and I felt rested like I had a good night's sleep.

That morning I went to visit my friend Jenice. Her house was welcoming and she always had food ready if she knew I was coming. She was a keen gardener, which could be seen by her beautiful, immaculate gardens. Together we walked to the back garden and she handed me a glass of juice as we sat under the shade of the swinging chair.

"So Beth, what is going on? How are you settling in at the house?" she asked. I shared with her the constant sense of evil that appeared to be around me since I moved back to my father's house.

"It's so difficult living there," I sighed deeply, "Oh Jenice, what have I let myself into?" I blinked my eyes shut to stop the tears. I was fed up of crying.

"I hear you Beth, but don't worry you're doing good. Wait there a moment." She went into the house and came back carrying her Bible and placed it on the table, "God's word acts as your defence. It's like a sword fighting on your behalf. Every time Satan comes to attack you with nightmares, depression or cause you to be fearful, God's word acts as your protection. It is powerful and sharper than any two-edged sword. Satan can't fight against that kind of power," she said excitedly, moving her hands like she was sword-fighting.

"Satan? What's he got to do with anything?" I questioned, still amused by her animated response.

"Him 'av everyting fi do wid it," she said going off into her patois, making me laugh.

"You know something Jenice, as a child growing up in church I heard about Satan, they sometimes called him the devil. We sang Sunday school rhymes about him and his fight to try and get us to follow him and not Jesus. It's funny, I remember this elderly lady at church, if she dropped anything she would say, 'look what the devil make me do now!' And Mrs May, she always said 'You see that devil, when I came through the door this morning, he make me trip and fall down, but God always pick me up," I said laughing. "I could never understand why they brought him to church if he caused them so much trouble!" I added as Jenice and I laughed uncontrollably.

"You're too funny Beth. It's serious business though," Jenice said suddenly, in a solemn tone, her expression making me laugh even more. I soon realised that she was really serious and composed myself, wiping the laughter tears from my eyes.

"Come on Jen, Satan is just church nursery rhymes I learnt at Sunday school. Why would he bother about me? I'm not convinced he's even real, and besides I've never done anything to him, so why would he be so keen on messing with my life?"

"Come let me show you," she said taking her Bible off the table and sitting next to me. Jenice showed me how Satan had a very important position in heaven until he messed up. He wanted the glory and the praise God was getting, so he conspired with some angels to remove God from power and take control. Satan soon found out how powerful God was when He threw him and his conspirators out of heaven. Since then Satan spends all his time trying to get people to worship him instead of God and attacks anyone who chooses God over him.

"Since you have chosen to be part of God's family, by asking Jesus into your heart, Satan is now angry with you. He will try anything to get you to give up the relationship with Jesus and 'fear' is one of his best strategies." Jenice said, handing me a book.

"What's this about?" I said reading the title.

"Just something to read, to help you get a better understanding of what may be going on around you at this time. Remember that God's Word says fear brings torment."

"Torment, you make it sound sort of scary!" I wiggled my fingers and pulled a scary face.

"This is no joke Beth! Torment is one of the characters of fear. You moved back to your father's house where fear was a stronghold. You lived in fear of your father as a child and he feared what others would say or think if the Pastor's kids misbehaved," she said.

"You are right," I thought about the fear of the abuse I lived with for many years, but this was something I didn't want to talk about. "I've got to go Jen before the carer leaves."

"Remember Beth, fear never comes by itself. It also comes with anxiety, stress and worry, which come with another load of baggage all of their own," she said as we walked to the door.

"That must be why Jesus keeps telling me not to worry and not to fear so many times. But Jen, I don't want Satan to be my priority, it's not like I want a relationship with him or anything. I just need to know enough to understand who or what I am dealing with," I said.

"I know Beth, but keep it in your mind that he's a smooth-talking salesperson who offers you goods on loan, with a very high interest rate and the consequences of non-payment are fatal," she replied. "Come dear let me pray for you before you go," she said holding my hands.

As I drove home, I reflected on my conversation with Jenice. Yes Satan may be real, but I also knew Jesus was real. He had become my focus and there were so many new and exciting things to discover about Him, and there was His Father to meet! There was no way I was going to give Satan my attention.

Chapter 10
Father

I accepted Jenice's invitation to a coffee evening at her house. I arrived to an atmosphere buzzing with happy chatter and laughter.

"Hi Beth, I'm so glad you could come," she hugged me and guided me in the direction of the kitchen. "Come let's get a drink," she clicked the kettle, "what would you like tea or coffee?"

"Tea please."

"Help yourself to one of those," she prompted pointing at some pretty decorated cupcakes.

"There's a lot of people here Jen," I said taking a cupcake as she handed me a warm mug.

"Yes I try to have a little get together every once in a while," she said holding my arm. "Let me introduce you to a special friend of mine," she said as she gently pulled me through the cluster of people in the corridor. I dodged and turned trying not to spill my tea.

"Mark, this is Beth," she said smiling from ear to ear.

"Hello Beth, nice to meet you," a small set, dark-skinned man shook my hand. His voice was so soft and calm with an African accent.

"Nice to meet you too," I smiled nervously.

"This is my friend I told you about who designs the most amazing wedding dresses," she said proudly and excused herself, leaving me to carry on a conversation with Mark. There was an awkward silence, and then we both started talking at the same time, causing us both to laugh. I was beginning to relax into the conversation when Jenice clapped her hands, calling everyone together.

"Thank you all for coming and I hope you are all enjoying yourselves," she smiled, walking across the room to pick up a Bible, her elegant, blue knee length dress, swaying as she moved. "We are going to have a short time of praise and thanksgiving before we go," she announced. Everyone made themselves comfortable, some sitting on chairs and others on the floor, like they had all done this before. Jenice read a verse from the Bible.

"Would anyone like to share what this verse means to you?" she asked, looking straight at me. I glared back at her, narrowing my eyes *don't you even think about it, Jenice!* She gave me a mischievous smile and looked away as someone began to speak. When everybody had shared, Jen encouraged us all to pray. It was a little perplexing for me at first, I wasn't used to praying within earshot of others. But as they all started to pray, I sensed an awesome presence in the room. It seemed to affect everyone, causing some to kneel on the floor crying, and others to worship in a heavenly language. I felt a tingling sensation that started at the top of my head and ran all the way to my feet and instead of praying, I started laughing uncontrollably. I don't know how long this went on for, but no matter how much I tried to stop, I just couldn't.

At the end of the meeting, I felt a freedom that no words could express. I said my goodbyes and was about to leave when Mark came up to me.

"That was the joy of the Lord filling your heart, through the power of the Holy Spirit."

"Umm," I said creasing my brow, as my smile disappeared.

"Isn't it awesome!" he declared smiling.

"Isn't what awesome?" I whispered confused.

"When Holy Spirit comes in like that," he said clasping his hands together. "For that joy to remain, you must forgive your father and tell him you have forgiven him," he continued, still smiling. I was so shocked I froze to the spot, lost for words. I had never met or seen this man before that evening, and knew very little about him, so why did he say that? In my shaken state I turned and looked at him, his smile still in place.

"Why did you say that?" I responded abruptly. His smile faded as he noticed the puzzled look on my face.

"I..I'm not sure," he stammered, "I don't know your situation, but while we were praying that's what I felt Holy Spirit wanted me to tell you," he replied his brow wrinkled with concern. "Am I wrong?" he questioned.

"No, no, you're not wrong," I answered exhaling as I allowed my shoulders to relax. I wanted to ask him what he meant by 'Holy Spirit wanted me to tell you', but instead I apologised for being so abrupt, and after a short conversation I said goodnight and left. On the way home, Mark's words echoed in my mind. *Who was this Holy Spirit he talked about anyway?* The only Holy Spirit I had heard about made people behave strange and fall all over the place and I sure didn't see that happening tonight! *Who was He, and when did He come to the meeting to give this person such a personal message for me?* I couldn't wait to get home to talk to Jesus about this.

When I arrived home, I went to my room and entered the throne room of my heart. He stretched His arms out towards me, with a smile on His face. I embraced Him and then knelt by His feet. He looked into my eyes and waited for me to speak.

"Who is Holy Spirit?" I asked.

"He is the one I sent to help you, when I left earth and came back to my Father in Heaven. He has taken my place to be with you, just like I was with the disciples when I was on earth."

"But, isn't He the one that causes people to jump all over the place and fall over," I responded more confused than before.

"Nooo!" He chuckled, "He is the one that tells you the truth about my Father and the kingdom of Heaven. Everything Father wants you to know, He tells Holy

Spirit and Holy Spirit explains it to you, in a way that you can understand. He comforts you when you are sick and lonely, He shows you how to do things you struggle with, and He will guide you when you have difficult decisions to make. He understands when you are sad and laughs with you when you are happy."

"Hmm, I don't get it! Where does He live then?"

"Right here in your heart. He is the part of me that goes with you everywhere. You can talk to Holy Spirit wherever you are, at anytime. You don't have to wait to come into the throne room of your heart to talk to me. As you read my Word - the Bible, He will help you to understand who He is." Jesus looked at my puzzled expression and gently tilted my chin, "Beth, He is already in you, you just don't recognise Him yet, but you will! From the moment you invited me into your heart, Holy Spirit came too," He said. Now this was just too much to take in!

"Okay…But how will I know it's Him?" I asked trying to be patient and trying to understand.

"You will know and recognise Him by His voice. He is the voice of truth and He sounds just like me. Talk to Him, He will answer all your questions about Himself and about my Father's kingdom," Jesus smiled.

"Oh, ok," I said getting up to leave, still quite unsure.

"And don't forget to talk to your father," He said as I walked to the door.

"Okay!" I said walking into my room.

I didn't fully understand why it took two people to help me run my life, three if you included His Father! But

I promised Jesus I would trust Him, so I asked Holy Spirit to show up for me. I looked around waiting for Him to turn up, but I couldn't see Him anywhere. *The question is, would I recognise Him even if He did?* Mark said that Holy Spirit talked to him and it was Holy Spirit that gave me so much joy and laughter at Jenice's house. *So where was He now!*

"I will have to trust you Jesus, on this Holy Spirit person turning up. After all He's your family," I said out loud.

It was getting late and I couldn't wait any longer for Holy Spirit to appear, so I knocked on my father's bedroom door. As soon as my knuckle tapped the door, I regretted it. I hadn't thought this through. *What on earth am I going to say?*

"Beth you are so impulsive," I frowned, as a feeling of fear drove in like a policeman on a motorbike. My heart raced into flight mode, my mouth went dry like I had just eaten chalk, but there was no turning back, my father had answered my knock.

"Come in," he said, his voice low and tired.

I put my head round the door and hesitated before entering, hoping Holy Spirit would breeze in. My father's room was dimly lit and he was perched at the end of his bed. I noticed how weak and frail he was getting.

"Come in," he repeated when he saw my hesitation. I pushed the door further open and went into his room, still holding onto the door handle.

"Sorry for disturbing you. I...I can see you are ready for bed," I stuttered, "but can we talk?" I asked trying to ignore the surprised expression on his face. "It won't take a minute," I confirmed.

"Well talk," he said sharply. "It must be important if you want to talk," he jived.

"Yes I think it's important," I replied as my stomach turned a somersault. *Come on Beth, get a grip,* I scolded.

"I am in the process of finding out more about Jesus and Holy Spirit..."

"You were brought up in church and now you're telling me you don't know who Jesus and Holy Spirit are?" he snapped, raising his eyebrows before I could explain.

"I know the religion of who they are, but I want to know them personally, but part of getting to know them is to learn to forgive," I said quickly.

"Forgive! Then find whoever you have to forgive!" he replied with a sly smile.

"But it's you. I...I need to forgive you," I said tentatively. His facial expression changed from amused to offended. I seemed to have touched a raw nerve. The atmosphere became tense.

"What do you mean? Needing to forgive me!" he boomed. "What have I ever done to you that you need to forgive?" His eyes widened with anger. He stood to his feet and walked to the other side of the room and sat heavily on the chair. My heart sank as it began to thump into my chest. I wanted to escape as his words echoed in my head.

I could think of a hundred things I need to forgive you for right now, my mind argued back, but instead I heard myself say, "I don't think it would do you or me any good to go back and rake up the conversations we should have had years ago," I responded with boldness. "I have obviously said something that hurt you and I'm sorry, but for me to be free, I must forgive and let you know that I have forgiven you," I continued. I let go of the door handle that was now digging into my hand, from the tight grip I depended on to hold me up, as a feeling of guilt grabbed me.

He waved at me to leave the room, his hands shaking, and the conversation ended right there. I stumbled into my bedroom. *I wasn't asking him to forgive me! I was telling him I forgave him! So what was the problem?*

I lay on my bed as my father's words continued to roll over and over in my head and a dark feeling of depression fell on me like a heavy blanket. I didn't mean to upset him, I just wanted to make things right! I tossed and turned regurgitating every word of the conversation trying to figure out what I said that was so wrong. Tears of frustration trickled down the side of my face as I turned staring at the white walls, trying to still my thoughts to think more clearly. Suddenly my white wall began to change colour to a mass of grey dust, followed by a loud sound of horses' hooves. I slowly eased my head off the bed blinking to check if this was really happening, when an army of guilt and shame burst through the grey dust like soldiers. They were riding on black horses, dressed in ancient black armoury, metal spears at the ready, galloping towards me shouting a war cry. The sound vibrated through my body and I tried to sit up. Fear pinned me to the bed, as the lead soldier charged with his spear, ready to pierce my chest. I tried to scream, but no sound would come out.

I whispered, "Jesus, help me," and as the words left my lips, an invisible shield appeared between me and the spear. The metal hit the shield making a sound like lightning whipping through the sky. I sat in stunned silence as the soldiers and their horses disappeared back into the wall.

This battle is not yours, it is mine. I will never leave you. Nothing will by any means harm you.

I cried in relief realising that Jesus was right there with me and His Words took the place of my father's voice. The tears turned into irrepressible sobs as the heavy blanket of gloom lifted. My eyes began to close as the tears subsided and I fell into a restful sleep.

A few weeks later my father called me into his room. He was sitting in his chair by the window as he often did.

"I'm not feeling well," he told me.

"What's wrong?" I asked, "Do you need a doctor?" I probed.

"I'm not sure," he replied looking up at me.

"I can't help you if you don't give me something to work with," I said, getting a little irritated. It was getting late and I needed to get to the studio. He had been doing this once too often now and even the carers were getting bored with it.

"Dad I really need to go," I sighed.

"I…I need you to forgive me," he stammered. His words took me completely by surprise.

"Me, forgive you!" I was flabbergasted. I looked at his anxious face and realized that it must have taken every ounce of courage within him to say those words, and my heart melted. "Of course I forgive you." I hugged him for the very first time and the chains of resentment, bitterness and anger snapped. I could hear as they clinked to the floor. There was a feeling of emotional release, like someone had lifted a heavy weight from my shoulders. I'm not sure what happened that morning and I can't say I really understood, but something changed within me. He didn't say he was sorry for the way he treated me or that he loved me, he didn't even hug me, but at that moment it didn't seem to matter. *Was this the beginning of a relationship that Jesus told me about?*

My relationship with my father did not become perfect overnight and was tested many times after this. His words didn't often match up with his actions and my resolve to accept him as an imperfect person was often difficult. Consequently when Jesus told me He wanted me to meet His Father, I was hesitant. I remember the day like it was yesterday. I went into the throne room to talk with Jesus. We laughed and chatted as I danced in worship.

"I want you to meet Father today," He said quite casually.

"Your Father!?" my stomach twisted.

"Yes, my Father," He smiled.

"Err... I don't think I'm ready for that!" My mouth went dry and I eyed the throne room door ready to retreat if necessary.

"Oh come on Beth, of course you are. Look how long

we've known each other. I've told Him so much about you and He can't wait to meet you."

There was an excitement in Jesus' voice as He spoke and I didn't want to disappoint Him, so I agreed to go. He led me through to some stairs, in a corner of the garden I had never noticed before. As we ascended I saw a beautiful mahogany door, with carvings of doves, trumpets and other musical instruments. There was a change of atmosphere, which caused me to feel weak at the knees. I stopped and gasped for air.

"I can't go any further," I said sitting on the step. The air was filled with an aroma that reminded me of sweet jasmine, honeysuckle and roses. It made me feel light-headed, like I was floating, not walking. "What's wrong with me? I can't seem to stand up!" I said, but in my heavenly language, which unsettled me even more. Jesus smiled at me. The atmosphere didn't appear to affect Him.

"It is the presence of Father. He has this effect on people. All the angels are worshipping. The sweet aroma is the praise and worship of all Father's children. You will get used to it as you come to Him more often."

He held my hand and I continued up the stairs with Him. When we got to the top I noticed that the door that appeared wooden and beautifully carved, was now transparent. We walked through into the Royal Throne Room. I cannot explain the awesomeness of what I heard and saw. There were angels everywhere just worshipping. A brightness obscured my vision of the room and I fell on my knees, joining the angels in worship. Jesus left me and went up to the throne, leaning on the armrest as He casually spoke to His Father.

"I've brought her to meet you," He was excited.

"Where did you meet her?" His Father asked.

"At the cross when I was crucified. I saw her there and when our eyes met I knew she would be mine," His eyes twinkling with love. "Then we met many times in the garden and in the throne room of her heart. I love her Father and I want her as my bride," He said with conviction.

"Go and bring her to me," I heard His Father say. Jesus obediently came over to where I was bowed face down in worship.

"Beth, Beth!" I looked up in response to His voice. His hand was frantically moving backward and forward. "Come over here, Father wants to talk to you," He waved His hands beckoning me to come. I struggled to my feet, passed the angels and stood by Jesus. He held my hand and led me to His Father. I noticed my fear had gone, replaced with a joy and a boldness I could not explain. I bowed before Him in reverence as He spoke.

"Jesus has told me many things about you and as you know, He loves you very much," He said. Jesus put His arms around my shoulders as His Father continued, "I love you Beth, more than you can ever know. Everything I have is yours. You can come with Jesus any time. Welcome to the family!" He exclaimed as He threw His arms around me and gave the biggest hug. Resting in His arms, I was confident that He was going to be the Father I had always wished for. His voice was tender just like

Jesus'. He was nothing like my father. I thanked Father and then Jesus said it was time to go. We walked out of the throne room into daylight.

I woke up with a feeling of exhilaration. I sat at my dressing table, picked up my comb and began to untangle my long hair. I couldn't help but smile at myself in the mirror. I had met Father, really met Him, and He was amazing. All my fears of meeting Him were completely unfounded. He wasn't angry, and His loving eyes showed no hint of disappointment. He said He loved me. I thought about the brides that came to my studio, many with issues concerning their father that caused emotional problems when getting married.

"If only they could meet Him too," I said into the mirror.

There's no reason why they can't.

I sat contemplating. I supposed there was no reason why they couldn't feel the way I felt right now. Privileged, that's how I felt, like I was the only person in the world who knew this secret - that Father was awesome, and He loved ME! I laughed into the mirror. *Me, He loves me!*

You are His and He is yours.

I narrowed my eyes, and with my newfound boldness I asked, "Is that you Holy Spirit?"

Chapter 11
Designer

I waited in the stillness of my room to hear His voice. I took a deep breath, trying not to make a sound, just in case I missed Him. Slowly turning myself on the chair, I looked around the room. He was right there, I could sense Him, but the room remained still.

"I know it is you Holy Spirit, Jesus said you would come."

"Of course it's me. Don't you recognise my voice?" He whispered softly. I tried to remain still, I was talking to Holy Spirit, the same way I would Jesus. But I almost felt that if I raised my voice too loud, He would drift away. I thought I heard Him laugh – *maybe he heard my thoughts?*

"I'm not going anywhere, Beth. You are right, you can talk to me in the same way you talk to Jesus. We are all one God - Father, Son and me, Holy Spirit." I shook my head - that was impossible. *How could they be one?* I had met each person separately.

"Think of water. One substance, however it can take the form of ice when frozen, liquid when defrosted, and a vapour when it is heated."

I smiled, "That makes sense, but I can see Jesus in the throne room of my heart and I met Father. I can't see you."

"Are you sure you've never seen me?"

"The rain!" I exclaimed, "In my studio that day, I saw the ceiling open and rain come through." I thought back to how drenched I had felt one moment and then completely dry the next. "Was that you?" I said slowly.

I didn't hear His voice, but my heart felt as though it echoed a response. Of course it was Him. My mind started to race with all the times I had felt Him, I had heard Him. I had been completely oblivious to His existence.

"So, the day I was at Jenice's house and laughed in worship - that was you!" I said putting my hand over my mouth.

"Yes, and the day you stood outside your father's door, I was there. I helped you and your father have the courage to forgive."

"The garden...and the throne room of my heart? Did you help me see it?"

"Yes, I show you what is happening in the Spirit realm, and help you understand who Jesus and Father are."

I gasped. I had always thought that somehow I was

unique, sort of peculiar, because I could see things that others had never told me about.

"Everyone's relationship with me is different, and it is normal to see what I show you."

What a relief. I felt accepted. I had kept my relationship with Jesus a secret. I had trusted Raoul and told him that I often spoke with Jesus, and that had blown up in my face. Since then, I had made a conscious decision to keep my 'crazy' to myself.

"We've got a lot of work to do," Holy Spirit declared.

"We do?"

"Well, my beautiful Bride, you've got to prepare for your wedding."

I looked up sharply, "No offence, but what on earth are you talking about? I have no intention of getting married again - EVER! Have you not seen my life? Haven't you noticed men and I don't even get on right now!"

Silence. Well if Holy Spirit wasn't going to talk to me, I knew exactly where to go to get answers. A moment later I was in the throne room of my heart.

"Jesus," I declared loudly. He stepped down from the throne and slowly walked over to me. "Can you believe what Holy Spirit just said? He wants me to get married! How ridiculous? Don't you think?" Jesus smiled sweetly.

"Calm down Beth, it sounds like good advice to me."

My eyes grew wide and my jaw dropped open. Composing myself I folded my arms.

"Jesus I am not sure this relationship with Holy Spirit is going to work out, even you are talking strange now." Laughing, He angled His head to the side.

"This marriage would be different, you would be a Bride of Christ, my bride."

Stunned, I said nothing. Breathing slowly, I looked at Jesus. This was not happening. I had escaped my first marriage and barely held it together when Raoul left. Marriage held no positive experiences for me, and for the first time I wanted to run out of the throne room. I had to get back to reality.

"Jesus, this is too much for me to take in. I...I have to go, can we speak later?" Jesus nodded in response and I saw Him drop His head slightly. I had hurt Him.

I shuffled uneasily on my dressing table chair. I had to work this through. I didn't want to be without Jesus, and I didn't want to hurt Him, but marriage was never part of the deal.

To be a Bride of Christ is an honour.
Let me teach you.

Bible verses came flooding into my mind. Although I didn't really want to listen, I was compelled to search for them. I reached for my Bible.

"The Bride of Christ, is the church?" I asked Holy Spirit.

"Yes, you are the church. You are becoming prepared every day since you accepted Jesus into your heart, to become His Bride."

I sat back in my chair. *How could I become the Bride of Christ? I am not holy, and I am not spotless or without blemish. I was a mess most of the time!*

"I will teach you how to live right, and help you become prepared. There is nothing you can do to make yourself right before Father. You will have to learn to take on Christ's righteousness."

"Umm hum," I didn't understand, it all seemed complicated to me.

"Beth, I would be your Wedding Planner."

"Really...I'd have my own personal wedding planner?" I smiled relaxing slightly. Maybe this wouldn't be as bad as I thought, I understood wedding planning. I was part of that process when the brides were preparing for their weddings. A little excitement began to rise within me.

"Ok. Let me tell you about a woman called Esther." We sat together as we read the story of Esther.

"She must have been terrified going to that strange place and being forced to be someone she didn't want to be." My excitement began to fade.

"Yes she was, but she didn't know at the time that she was specially chosen to go to the palace."

"Am I specially chosen to be a Bride of Jesus?"

"Yes, even before you were born Father chose you to be part of His family and just like He had a plan for Esther's life, He has a plan for you."

"Really!" He now had my full attention.

"Just like Esther had Hagar to help her prepare for her special day, Jesus has asked me to help you."

Holy Spirit explained that Hagar the eunuch knew the king's habits, his likes and dislikes, what made him happy, what made him sad, his enemies and his friends. This qualified him to teach Esther and prepare her for the day when she would stand before the king. He taught her the correct way to present herself – how to speak, walk, dress and even what to eat.

"So in effect she had to learn a completely new way of life!" I stood to my feet, hands on hips. "How can that be right?"

"Beth, Hagar had to prepare her for where she was going, who she was to become. He was preparing her to be a bride. Not just any ordinary bride, but a bride of a king," He said as I paced the floor.

There was a tug of war going on inside of me. The memory of Jesus looking so hurt when I left the throne room caused my stomach to twist in knots. The last thing I wanted to do was hurt Him, in fact He had become my best friend. I sat next to Holy Spirit.

"I want Jesus and all that He is, but I'm not brave and strong like Esther." Holy Spirit reached over and dried the tears that rolled down my cheeks.

"Beth, I know Jesus and I know Father very well. I can help you and teach you how to live right, in order to prepare you to be the Bride you are called to be," He smiled, as He put His arms around my shoulders. "But you will have to trust me."

"Do you think, Jesus is angry with me, for not accepting His proposal to be His Bride?" I asked nervously.

"Not at all Beth, just speak to Him, right now. Let Him know how you feel."

"Jesus!" I shouted, fearing He wouldn't hear me because I wasn't in the throne room. "I'm sorry, I want to be your Bride!" I declared.

I began to include Holy Spirit in my life. I often asked Him to help me with difficult designs I had to do for the brides. He always showed me how to make intricate paper patterns I found difficult. At other times, He would direct me to where I could source unusual fabrics. He became my 'Personal Advisor'. I began to learn to listen carefully and hear His voice, especially when my life got hectic, and I'd try and do things my own way. The more I got to know Him, the easier it became to recognise it was Him speaking to me, and not my own conscience. Sometimes, it wasn't His voice I heard, but a nudging within me, which guided me, when I was unsure. He didn't condemn me or put me down every time I slipped up or made a mistake, but He gently prodded. He often showed me through the Bible or explained important lessons to me in a practical way, drawing on my experience as a designer. I was continually learning about His family principles and expectations and found that there was always something new to learn.

⚜

I arrived at the studio and was greeted by the postman.

"Is that for me?" I asked grinning from ear to ear.

"Yes," he said smiling back, "and good morning to you too," he said teasing.

"Oh, how rude of me! I was so excited about the package I forgot my manners, sorry," I said in a high-pitched voice. "Good morning and how are you today?" I continued.

"Much better now the sun is up," he replied. "I hope whatever is in that parcel was worth your wait. Enjoy!" he said as he waved and hurried to the next building.

I ran into the studio and tore the package open and there it was. The most stunning gold lace fabric I had ever seen or handled. It was very expensive and I was reluctant to even touch it. I cautiously laid it on the cutting table and carefully opened every fold. With every move the gems glistened in the light, twinkling, showing off its beauty, reminding me of its value and extravagance. I stood back, looking at it in admiration. *How could I ever take the scissors and cut through this work of art!* I sat heavily on the chair, captivated by the fine looking fabric.

"Oh Holy Spirit, how on earth am I going to cut this fabric?" I whispered.

"Beautiful isn't it!"

"Gorgeous!" I responded quietly, as if a loud noise would somehow disturb its splendour.

"But you know Beth, if you don't cut it to the pattern you have designed, as beautiful as it is, it wouldn't fulfil its purpose. The real beauty of this fabric will only show when you follow the pattern."

"Ok, I know, but just look at it! This isn't easy you know, and what if I make a mistake?" I deliberated.

"Umm, I know what you mean," He continued softly, "That fabric represents your life in a way. Let's just go back to the story of Esther for a moment. She had to go through many changes before she was ready to go before the king, and many more before she was ready to be a bride. She had to leave her family behind and life as she knew it, her culture, the way she dressed, the food she ate and the language she spoke, in order to learn a new one. Put it this way, like that fabric many things had to be cut away from her life, in order for her to be fit for the purpose she was designed for."

"It must have been really painful for her. I would not have made all those changes for a man, even if he were a king!"

Holy Spirit laughed, "You are making changes every day, Beth, look at the person you are today compared to this time last year. Step by step things in your life have been cut away, left behind and some beautiful qualities are developing within you."

I looked at the fabric as it lay on the table in all its extravagance. Jenny my 'bride to be' was due to arrive in two days for her first fitting, so I had no more time to be sentimental about this beautiful piece of fabric. It had a purpose - it was to adorn Jenny and make her feel like the most special person in the room on her wedding day. I looked at the design of the dress I had drawn and after anxiously studying it for a while, I hung it on the wall. Taking a deep breath to steady my hand, I took the scissors and began to cut. I then started pinning each piece together, positioning them on the dressmaker's dummy to ensure the pieces hung correctly. My heartbeat accelerated with excitement as I tacked each seam and the dress began to take shape. The fabric was now coming alive and looked more beautiful than ever. I placed the gown on the dress form and stood back in amazement! I now began to understand what Holy Spirit meant when He said, "The real beauty of this fabric will only show, when you follow the design and cut out the pattern."

As I tidied the studio that evening, I examined the leftover pieces of fabric and thought how useful they would be to make a bodice or a short skirt. I folded the material and put it on the shelf. I was very tired and asked Holy Spirit to help me tidy up. I was about to throw away the small, insignificant pieces when Holy Spirit stopped me. I took the scraps and laid them on the table.

"What do you see?"

"Lovely, but very small pieces of fabric," I replied shrugging my shoulders. "What do you see?" I enquired.

"Potential," He replied turning to look at me, "Even the smallest piece of fabric can be used for something. This little piece could be used to make a handbag, or even decorate a picture frame, but because it was cut away from the bigger piece, it appears to have lost its significance. Your past experiences can often make you feel small and insignificant," He continued.

I held up the small piece of fabric up in the light. *Yes, I could do something with this.*

"You're right I could create a make-up bag with this bit."

"Exactly, it isn't a useless piece of fabric anymore. Life can often leave you feeling cut up and discarded. Jesus knows how to use each of those life experiences no matter how small, broken or cut up they are, and make something beautiful out of them. He is the greatest Designer!" He said, as I turned off the lights and locked the door.

That night as we were reading together, Holy Spirit showed me how God chose to elevate individuals who people think of as insignificant, because often they are the ones that are overlooked and considered weak. God doesn't see them that way. I silently said a prayer to Father, thanking Him, because I had felt like one of those individuals, but He chose me anyway.

Jenny arrived early and excited for her first fitting. That was until she saw the dress with all its uneven edges and straggly pieces of thread.

"It looks nothing like the drawing on the wall", she said, her forehead creased with disappointment, and her tone quickly turned to anger.

She told me in no uncertain terms how let down she felt, and was ready to walk away and leave me with the unfinished dress. When she finished venting her dissatisfaction, I quietly and calmly explained.

"Jenny I couldn't go any further with the dress until you had tried it on. At this stage it is easier and more practical to correct any faults. If I had finished it and it didn't fit perfectly, we would run the risk of damaging the fabric doing alterations." She was not convinced.

"What's the use of trying it on when it doesn't look anything like what I'd ordered?!" Her blue eyes shone with tears.

"Jenny, please just try it on. The dress wasn't made for the dummy it's on, it was made for you and it will look different when it's on you."

I continued to reassure her as she stepped into the dress that everything was going to plan and that she would have to trust me with the process. *Now where have I heard that before?* I thought to myself, as Jenny slipped into the dress. She was amazed at how different it looked on her.

"Wow! I wasn't expecting that!" she gasped covering her mouth. "I'm so sorry, Beth. I can see it's going to be amazing."

"That's ok, I understand."

We agreed another date for her second fitting and I asked her to bring the lingerie and shoes that she would be wearing on the day. She looked a little confused at my unusual request.

"I just want to make sure the dress fits perfectly with no lumps and bumps," I said with a little chuckle, thinking that's something I could imagine Holy Spirit saying.

"Ahh ok, good thinking," she said smiling.

Not long after my customer left, Holy Spirit came into the studio.

"How did the fitting go?" He asked casually. I turned and looked at Him a little surprised!

"You mean you didn't see or hear?" I asked, my voice going up and down in a surprised tone. I was still a little miffed by Jenny's negative reaction to what I thought was a beautiful creation, so my prickly response went unchecked.

"I am just asking your opinion on the fitting," He gently replied untouched by my retort.

"It was ok," I replied awkwardly, "but she expected the dress to look more like the design." I checked my tone of voice before finishing my sentence, "but I reassured her that by the next fitting she would recognise and identify with it more." I sat on the chair. *Surely He was there all the time, so why did He ask me?*

"Life gets like that sometimes, don't you think?" Holy Spirit said as He sat down next to me.

"Gets like what?" I asked with a puzzled frown.

"Like that wedding dress. Your life circumstances or your actions may not reflect the completed design, and the criticism of others may cause you to give up. In fact, it has caused many to break off their engagement to Jesus."

"What do you mean?" I asked, still puzzled by His comment.

"Like Jenny, you are often impatient. It's also upsetting when others have high expectations of you. They expect you to change and be perfect overnight, just like Jenny expected the dress to be perfect even before she had tried it on," He answered as he turned and looked at me.

"Yes! Like yesterday when Benji took my car without asking and made me angry and I…oh well you know what I said," I admitted, getting up and busying myself to avoid His gaze. "But then He had the cheek to say, "I thought you were kind and giving. You're a Christian," I continued mimicking Benji's voice.

"How did you feel when Benji said that?"

"Irritated," I replied flopping back on the chair. "I know he was trying to make light of the situation, but at the same time he had a point, which annoyed me even more. I was embarrassed that I got so angry at him and imagine what you and Jesus must have thought," I continued with a sigh.

"Jesus didn't mention it, because you are deeply loved and completely forgiven," He said quietly as a stillness settled in the studio.

"I'm totally forgiven, even when I mess up," I looked at Him with doubting eyes.

"Exactly. Jesus died on the cross once and for all, to ensure your sins are forgiven. He doesn't keep a score card every time you get it wrong, you know."

"Huh, does that mean I can do whatever I want!" I grinned.

"Well I suppose you could, but everything you do has consequences. I would suggest you stick to doing things that your heart says is right to do. It will make your life far easier. You don't want to be cleaning up mess from consequences, because you wanted to live your own way. But the decision is always yours."

Chapter 12
Change

Two weeks later Jenny arrived at the studio for her final fitting. This time I invited Holy Spirit to stay with me throughout the appointment. I had worked hard on the dress and hoped that Jenny would be pleased with its progress. As she came into the studio, the dress was set up on the display dummy under the light, to show it off in all its beauty. It shimmered as each crystal sparkled with light and colour.

"Oh my goodness!" she exclaimed as she covered her cheeks with both hands. "It is beautiful! More stunning now than I could have ever imagined!"

She walked around the dress, her hands glued to her face, catching each tear of joy that now fell continuously from her eyes. I handed her a tissue which took without looking.

"Wow, Beth!" she said catching her breath. She turned

to me and flung her arms around my neck, burying her head.

"How can I ever thank you?" her voice muffled by my shoulder.

"We can start by you trying it on," I replied teasing. I led her to the changing room, as though tearing her away from someone she couldn't bear to leave.

"Did you remember your underwear and your shoes?" I asked, as I shut the curtain to give her some privacy and time to compose herself.

"Yes, but you will have to help me do it up."

After a while I went to the changing room to assist with her Victorian Basque, but instead of laces there were what seemed to be hundreds of hooks. I pulled and tugged as I fastened it up and after many 'ouches' and 'ows' it was done.

"The pains we go through just to look a few pounds smaller in some places and bigger in others!" I said, as we both burst out laughing.

"I know, but in all seriousness, if I had continued with my exercise I wouldn't be going through all this tugging and pulling!" she said regrettably as she stepped into the netted petticoat.

I carefully removed the dress from the dummy, took it to the changing room and helped Jenny put it on. It fitted like a glove. I fought back a tear as I placed the tiara and a veil on her head and led her to the big mirror in the studio. She was speechless!

"You look amazing Jenny!" I said slowly, as we both stared at her reflection in the mirror.

"Is that really me?" she asked in a whisper, as tears filled her eyes again.

"Yes, that's you," I replied quietly, trying not to disturb her moment of awe.

"It's beautiful, so beautiful! Thank you, I feel a million dollars," she said taking another tissue to dry her tears.

Jenny took her time admiring herself in the mirror, turning left and right, looking at the dress from every angle and eventually agreed that it was time to take it off.

"Oh! And there is my 'something blue' I have to wear. I think I will get a blue garter, do you sell them here?" she asked as I helped her take off the dress.

"No. Sorry," I walked out of the changing room, leaving her to get dressed.

"Never mind, I may be able to borrow one from my friend and that will give me my 'something borrowed' and 'something blue' at the same time!" she said standing at the mirror, combing her hair back into style.

"Why do you need to borrow something and have something blue?" I asked curiously, as I hung the dress on a padded white satin hanger and placed it in a long gold and white dress bag.

"No special reason, just tradition I suppose," she replied looking at me strangely. "Why do you ask?"

"Just curious, it would be good to know what it's for or what it means," I replied, zipping up the bag and handing it to her. "It would be more meaningful if you knew what it meant."

"Oh Beth, don't spoil my fun now! We will go into this another time," she said casually, slightly annoyed that

I had challenged her. After carefully putting everything into the boot and laying her precious dress on the back seat, we said our goodbyes.

"Oh Holy Spirit, didn't she look beautiful?" I asked as I sat down holding a cup of tea in my hands.

"Umm, beautiful," He replied reflectively. "It reminds me of the dress Jesus and I have designed for your special day. The pattern is already cut and we are in the process of putting it together. It is even more beautiful than Jenny's dress, nothing like you have ever seen before and completely unique to you. Just like Jenny's dress wouldn't necessarily fit you, your garment wouldn't fit anyone else, not even your twin sister," He said as He turned and looked at me.

Intrigued I asked, "You are making me a dress?" *Finally, being a Bride, is becoming interesting again,* I smiled to myself. I couldn't imagine any dress more beautiful than Jenny's, but then I thought that of most of the wedding dresses I had made.

"So can you describe the dress? What kind of fabric is it made from?" I continued trying hard to contain my excitement.

"Get your Bible and I will show you," He said pointing to the shelf my Bible was on. I quickly stood up and took it down. "The fabric is made from total love and commitment, entwined with the thread of trust and obedience. It is adorned with pearls of peace, sprinkled with the clear crystals of joy that sparkle in the radiance of the Son. Underneath is the lining of forgiveness that holds out the dress in perfect shape," His eyes twinkled as He spoke.

"As beautiful as it sounds Holy Spirit, it doesn't sound like a normal wedding dress!" I replied, trying to take it all in and hide my disappointment. "What about the lingerie? Did you sort that out as well? I'd love a Victorian Basque like Jenny's," I said, hoping that it would be something beautiful that would enhance my figure.

"Ah don't worry about lingerie, Beth," He smiled. "Why would you need a painful basque, when you are developing a wonderful figure right now?"

I looked at myself in the long mirror. *This figure could do with some work.* I thought about the personal trainer I did my exercise workouts with. He sure worked me hard, but even he would agree with me.

"I'm talking about your spiritual figure Beth, you are taking on the nature of Jesus more and more every day. Each time we meet, you are doing a spiritual workout and by the time you are ready, your wedding dress will fit you perfectly, without the need for a basque."

He was right, I was changing day by day. Sometimes, I didn't recognise myself and, other times it felt like I was back to square one learning the basics again.

"This spiritual workout is serious hard work, Holy Spirit. Sometimes I wish I could just take a pill and be the perfect bride I long to be." I twirled in the mirror.

"Yes, it is challenging but don't be disheartened. Remember there are also the flowers of hope that bloom as you believe, and resting on your head is the crown of truth, made for you by Father. Then there are the shoes that run to tell others about Jesus, tied with the golden cord of faithfulness and service. On your finger you will wear the ring of honour. With all this, Father never takes away your ability to choose."

I wasn't sure that I was worthy or even strong enough to wear this splendid garment that Holy Spirit was designing for me.

"So what about something borrowed and something blue?" I asked curiously.

"Oh that!" He said His forehead creased with serious lines.

"Jenny appears to think it's an important tradition," I responded as a matter of fact.

"There are many wedding traditions that are not necessary for you. Traditions like wearing or carrying something old, new, borrowed and blue, carrying the bride over the doorway and jumping the broom, are all to do with warding off evil spirits from harming the bride and groom. Satan and his evil spirits, cannot harm you. You have invited Jesus into your life, so you have the whole of heaven protecting you, including an army of angels, to defend you."

"That is such a relief! I have my own army of angels. I'm royalty," I laughed and danced around the studio.

"Well technically you are, Beth. You are the daughter of a King, with all the benefits and privileges. Everything He has is yours." Holy Spirit beamed.

"Really! I was just kidding!"

"By the time I'm finished with you, you will be walking tall and talking like the Princess you are!"

I smiled, hoping that what Holy Spirit said was true, but deep down, I was not entirely convinced.

"Mom, these figures just don't add up."

"It's not all about money Mia, things will pick up."

"Yes we said that last month, but I'm serious, you are putting too much of your money into the business to keep it afloat."

I sighed, she didn't understand how much the studio meant to me, meant to the brides.

"Mom I know you love the studio, I do too, but we have to be realistic. You work so hard on the designs, but you will have to charge much more to justify the hours you put in."

She was right, I knew she was right. I had thought about it a lot this past month, but I wasn't ready to let go. This was my dream.

Reluctantly, I returned to the studio and slowly opened the door. I was savouring every moment, taking in everything about the studio that had become a second home to me. I stood in the middle of the shop floor and spun around. I loved this place, it was a part of me, part of who I had become, part of my freedom as a business woman. This was where I had met with Jesus and Holy Spirit countless times. When the chaos of home began to get on top of me, I would escape to my studio and reflect with Holy Spirit. Although I had known for months that the studio was losing money and it was time to close its doors, I had pretended it wasn't happening and just put it to the back of my mind. It was like losing a baby, someone that I loved. *I have put so much hard work into this business! I have put so much of myself into it! There's got to be another way?* I stomped the floor in frustration.

"I'm not ready to let go Holy Spirit, this is my studio!" I thumped the air with my fist, and then deflated I dropped it to the side of my body.

Getting angry at Him is pointless, I always end up apologising anyway! I looked around at my creations, my designs and I felt a surge of mixed emotions well up inside of me. I pursed my lips together. *No, I am not going to lose it today. Holy Spirit, Help!*

Benji and I spent the next few weeks, clearing out the studio of all the dresses, equipment, and packing away everything that the studio had represented. We stood looking at the many boxes that had filled the once organised studio.

"Where are you gonna put it all Mom, Grandad is not gonna be happy to have it all at his?"

Benji was right. *What was I going to do with it all?* I slumped down on one of the boxes. A loud ring made both me and Benji jump, and then laugh as we caught our breath.

"Benj I thought you had disconnected that phone," I narrowed my eyes at him as I walked over to the phone.

"I forgot!" I heard him shout as I lifted the receiver.

"Hello Beth's Studio," I gulped as I realised that would be the last time I'd be saying those words again, "Can I help you?"

"Hi Beth," a cheery voice came through the phone,

interrupting my upset thoughts. "Beth, it's me, Naomi."

"Oh hi Hun. Forgive me, I'm all over the place. How are you?"

"I'm fine, more importantly how are you? It's a big day for you."

"Yes," I sighed audibly, "There are boxes everywhere, it's just a mess, and I know my Dad is not going to want me to dump it all in his spare room. You know when you're just not in the mood for the hassle and the fight. Uh!"

"Well, I have a spare room, why don't you just bring it all here? I don't use the room anyway."

"Really!" I exclaimed, then caught myself, "Oh no Naomi, I couldn't impose on you like that. Thanks anyway."

"Beth, I mean it, bring it here, I don't mind and you wouldn't be imposing on me. The room is already cleared."

This could solve all my problems, I thought to myself, And I won't have to argue with Dad.

"You know what Naomi, thank you, I will take you up on that offer, if you're sure?" I was slightly uncomfortable but Naomi was a good friend, and had always helped me out when I needed it.

The early evening sun shone brightly as I turned the key to lock the studio for the last time. It was the end of another chapter in my life and I wasn't sure how to deal with it. I had no idea what I was going to do, but I knew I had to do 'something'. I decided to leave my parked car and go for a walk. I needed to clear my head, to think.

Jesus, what is next? I'm back at the beginning again! I began to walk aimlessly down the long street, and then stood in front of the big wedding shop on the main road. I had driven past this shop every day on the way to my studio. It had an enviable position on the street, and was my main competitor. I stopped to look at the wedding dresses in the window, as I always did. An irritation rose within me. *Look how basic their dresses are, and I put so much effort into mine. It's not fair!* As I glared at one of the dresses, that seemed to announce my failure, I noticed a small handwritten sign that read,

'Part-time shop assistant needed.
Apply within.'

To add insult to injury, I was closing my studio and they were hiring. I turned to walk away and felt Holy Spirit nudge me.

"Go on then!" He prompted.

"Oh nooo!" I quickly responded, "You have got to be kidding me. You expect me to work for a wedding shop, THAT wedding shop," I pointed towards the door, "No way. They were probably the reason I had to close my studio," I said taking a few steps away from the window.

"Beth, trust me. This is your answer to that 'something' to do," He said with a smile.

"Holy Spirit, are you telling me you couldn't find me something a little different from what I have just left!"

"That's why it is perfect for you. You know this business better than anyone, use your expertise to help someone else."

I sighed throwing my head backwards. He was right of

course. If I had been offered some help from someone who had expertise, maybe I wouldn't be standing here on the street considering taking this position. Before I could stop myself, I pushed the door open and went in.

I was greeted at the door by a woman. She was smartly dressed in a black trousers suit, complimented with a white chiffon blouse and low heeled black shoes. The black suit was in sharp contrast to her pale skin and brown hair, with blonde streaks that gave her a modern look.

"Hello, I'm Tracy. What can I do for you?" Her voice was calm and mature, her manner relaxed and welcoming. I explained that I had seen the advert in the shop window and wished to apply for the job. She invited me in and showed me to a chair. We sat talking for awhile and she explained that she was closing her shop and the job would only be temporary, until the end of the year.

"You are closing all of this?" I looked around, "I'm surprised, you have all this space, and you have a perfect view from the street. I bet you get a lot of passing trade," I looked at her enquiringly.

"I have been here about 18 months, but I am struggling to see a profit. The footfall is not as great as I would have hoped. And this big space comes at a big price." I could hear the disappointment in her voice, and understood exactly how she felt. A tinge of guilt filled me. I had been reluctant to even come into her shop, and had always seen it as a threat. To think she had been experiencing the same thing I had. Maybe I wasn't a failure after all.

"I have just closed my bridal studio," I admitted, "today actually. I understand exactly what you mean, there just isn't the demand in this area anymore." I had found someone who understood me, and at that moment realised why Holy Spirit had told me to come into her shop.

I left feeling lighter, almost as if I had shared part of my burden with her, and she with me. *Holy Spirit you are amazing, thank you.* My pace was quicker as I walked back up the road towards my car. I had nothing to worry about, Jesus had provided me with a job, the day my business closed. I laughed to myself as I got into my car, and breathed a deep sigh of relief.

That night I lay in bed tossing and turning with the day's events, still a little shocked by my spontaneous reaction in walking into the wedding shop and getting the job. As I turned for the umpteenth time, I caught a glimpse of the studio keys sitting cold and still on the top of my bag. I was due to hand them over to a representative from the City Council Monday morning. My earlier triumph did not detract from the fact that my bridal studio was closed. I felt sick in my stomach as the words *'I've failed again'* echoed through my mind. No sooner had that thought faded, then another would follow in quick succession, *'No I haven't failed'*. Over and over like a battle in mind. In an effort to shut out the voices I said out loud,

"It's time for a change that's all!" But who was I trying to convince? Even as the words left my lips I knew that I didn't want change. I had change all my life and it wasn't exciting anymore. Reaching out I took the keys, unzipped my bag and dropped them in. I couldn't bear to look at them or entertain the negatives they represented.

"Oh Jesus, I really need some sleep tonight, help me please," I whispered. In my attempt to get comfortable, I turned on my back and as I looked up, it was as if words gently floated from the ceiling and rested on my bed. Peace, calm, comfort, love, joy, happiness, rest, contentment, and as each word fell, it formed a blanket over me and I fell asleep.

Monday morning came all too quickly. It was raining as I got out of my car and hurried to the studio. The council representative was walking up to the studio door as I arrived.

"I'm sorry things didn't work out for you," he said, as the keys dropped into his hands.

"I'm sorry too, but maybe it's time for change," I responded, trying to sound as upbeat as I could. We walked out of the studio and he locked the door and hurried to his car as he said goodbye. I put up my umbrella and stood frozen to the spot. Wave after wave of negative emotions threatened to knock me off my feet and bury me in a sea of tears. *I've failed again.*

You only fail if you give up and stop trying.

I nodded acknowledging Holy Spirit. I wasn't giving up but the thought of embracing something new was scary. I walked slowly down towards the bridal shop and stood outside the door contemplating going right back home.

I am with you, go on in.

I pushed the door open, and heard the bell at the top of the door ring out, announcing my entrance.

"Hi Beth, good to see you. Come on in, I'll show you around." Tracy's upbeat chatter put me at ease. *Ok I'm going to try Holy Spirit, I might even enjoy myself.* Plastering a smile on my face, I greeted Tracy.

The shop was full of elegant dresses in different designs, colours, shapes and sizes. Tracy pointed out that the large window display would be my responsibility and must be changed every two weeks, with special care and attention to the seasonal displays. She took me to the reception area to show me the paperwork, the booking system and how the security worked. She informed me that she had an appointment the following morning, so I would need to open up the shop.

I woke early the following morning and sat on the edge of my bed for a while, trying to make sense of this new season in my life. My thoughts dragged along as I dressed and went downstairs to get some breakfast, but decided on just a hot drink. My stomach was filled with too many butterflies to fit food in as well. I stood by the window, looking out at the garden. Today was a new day and I was determined to give it my best shot. As I sipped the tea, I rehearsed the security code for the shop and the routine I was expected to follow, telling myself to get a grip as my heart missed a beat in fear of getting things wrong. I was determined it was not going to spoil my day, so I covered it up with make-up and a smile and left for work.

I had met Vera, the in-house seamstress the day before. We chatted while she shortened the hem of an ivory wedding dress. She was about three inches taller than me, with dark curly hair. Her voice was melodious as she spoke and no matter how annoying the dress alteration was, she just kept on smiling. Saturday was the busiest day of any wedding shop. Although we had an appointment system, customers always turned up spontaneously.

A group of women came into the shop. I wasn't sure which one was the 'bride to be' and from previous experience, I had learnt it was better to ask and not to guess! One of the ladies introduced herself and then motioned to Charlotte, the bride-to-be. Charlotte did not look like someone preparing for a wedding. There was no excitement in her voice and no smile on her face that was now bright red, as though she was embarrassed. There wasn't even a twinkle in her dark eyes, in fact she looked very unhappy. The excitement and chatter of her friends did not diminish her seeming sadness. I decided to look past her despondent face and encourage her to choose a few dresses on the rail that she liked. I then showed her into the changing room and helped her into one of the dresses. During our conversation she told me about the distressing time she had experienced at other wedding shops, and how she was treated with disrespect due to her size. I listened empathising with her, offering her a tissue to dry her tears as I tucked and pinned a modesty panel at the back of the dress she had chosen.

"How do I look?" she asked nervously.

"Lovely," I reassured encouraging her to clip her thick black hair up, as I placed a tiara on her head, and offered her some sample shoes to try on.

When she was ready, I took her back into the main shop and helped her onto a podium in the front of a full-length mirror. This was the first wedding gown she had ever put on, and as she looked in the mirror she gasped.

"Is that really me?"

"You look beautiful!" her sister exclaimed, as Charlotte spun around in excitement.

"I can't believe that I am actually in a wedding dress!" she cried, her eyes welling up with tears, but this time, they were tears of joy. For the first time she saw herself as a bride.

"You think you look incredible now, just think how amazing you would look in a brand new dress ordered exclusively for you," I said brightly.

My day was going well, I had secured my first sale and confidence was starting to grow inside me. *I really am good at this Holy Spirit.* I was doing what I knew best, and I hadn't expected it to make me feel so happy. I was still helping brides, and although it wasn't my shop, I still felt fulfilled.

Later that day a young woman came in for her final fitting accompanied by her mother. I hung the dress in the changing room and invited her in.

"No, no!" she said suddenly becoming distressed. I quickly removed my hands from the changing room curtains.

"I want my Mom to help me!" she said abruptly.

"No problem," I said calmly, "that is a good idea, especially if she is the one helping you on the day." I smiled as I got out of the way to allow her mother in.

"Just call if you need me."

I could hear their disapproving comments as I stood waiting. *What on earth is going on in that room?* It wasn't long before all was revealed.

"Look it doesn't fit!" her mother spat furiously, flicking her long blonde hair as she flung the curtains back, revealing a distraught and tearful bride. She was right. The dress appeared quite out of sorts, so I asked permission to lift the dress to check the lining and to make sure the net was properly pulled down.

"I'm afraid it doesn't fit because you haven't removed your jeans and top before putting on the dress," I informed them squeezing in my stomach trying not to burst out laughing. The look of embarrassment on their faces was a picture, but all I could think about was what if this had happened on her wedding day!

When the family left, Holy Spirit sat next to me still smiling from the episode of the appointment. I however, was not so amused.

"They were so rude," I said quietly.

"Ah, take no notice," Holy Spirit replied, gently nudging me in the ribs. "Come on smile!"

"Yes I guess you are right," I sighed, "if I was to take offence to every rude client that came into the shop, I would be a very unhappy person."

"You know Beth, there is a lesson to be learnt from that young lady," Holy Spirit said casually.

"What do you mean?"

"Some people, like that young lady often try to put on new things before taking off the old ones. There are some wonderful new changes happening for you, and more to come. You can't embrace them with your old mentality."

"Holy Spirit I have let go of so many things and people in my life, how much more is there to do? Look at Raoul, I really loved him, but I let him go."

"Yes, you make a good point. Men. How do you feel about them?"

"Honestly, I have too many things going on in my life right now to even think about them."

"Uh huh, but how will you accept a loving special relationship with a man, if you don't deal with the old relationships you have been in?"

Holy Spirit was right, of course. I hadn't even entertained the thought of having another man in my life, and the thought actually scared me. Being vulnerable to a man again, would be crazy. I had three men Father, Jesus and Holy Spirit, what more did I need?

Chapter 13
Trust

Time seems to move too fast when you are doing something you enjoy and before I knew it, the time had come for Tracy to close down the wedding shop. My season in the bridal business was now over, but as unsettling as it was when the shop doors closed, I was trusting that Father had something special up His sleeve for me. I was to find out much sooner than anticipated.

My new season started without work. Dad was back in hospital, which gave me a chance to sort out the house, and have a spring clean. I began giving away the fabrics from the studio that I no longer needed, to charities and schools.

"I'm sure they will be able to put it all to better use than me right now," I consoled myself, as I packed a black bag into my car boot. Leaning over to make room for another bag I felt my mobile vibrating in my back pocket. I reached down for it whilst balancing the bag on the edge of the boot. I didn't recognise the number that came up on the screen, it looked like it came from abroad.

"Hello," I said wondering who would be calling me from abroad.

"Hello, is that Beth?" a lady with a lively European accent came through the phone.

"Erm yes this is Beth...Can I help you?"

"Oh yes please, I have spoken with Tracy, she gave me your number. I need some help with a dress." She spoke so fast I struggled to catch all she was saying.

"Tracy, yes. Erm, ok, what sort of dress did you want?"

"I need a mother of the bride's dress for my daughter's wedding. Can you make it? You have come highly recommended." It sounded like she was smiling as she spoke.

"I'm sure I can help you. When is the wedding?"

"June, next month. We are in London at the moment and we will be leaving at the end of the week to go back to Italy."

"Ah right not much time. Would you be able to meet with me, so we can discuss exactly what you would like?"

We agreed to meet two days later. I called Benji, and he went to Naomi's house to retrieve all my sewing equipment and paperwork. I had to prepare a consultation from my father's house, which was a challenge. *Ok, I can do this,* I seemed to need to reassure myself often lately.

The day arrived, and I had prepared everything the best I could. I sat on the edge of the settee nervously awaiting the knock on the door. *Beth why are you so nervous, you've done this so many times before! Holy Spirit I need you at this meeting please.*

I knew He was there, but I still felt anxious with the anticipation of meeting them. When they finally arrived, my nervousness dissipated, as I welcomed a lively, warm and friendly family. The bride Sophia, her mother Ellen, who I had spoken to on the phone, her husband and the bride's brother, all bustled into Dad's living room, and began to tell me all about the wedding day they had planned. Ellen and I began to discuss exactly what she wanted from her mother of the bride dress along with animated input from all of the family. After collating all their ideas, I wrote down her measurements. They were due to come back in three days, to have a look at the fabrics I had sampled for them and also see the drawing of Ellen's dress design.

The next day, I had a distressing phone call from Ellen, as she hastily explained that the bride's dress they ordered from London had gone horribly wrong.

"Beth, I know this is a huge imposition but could you please make Sophia's dress? There's no time to order another one, it will not come in time for the wedding. I don't know what else to do."

Her voice sounded so distraught, I felt awful for them.

"Umm there isn't much time to do your dress and Sophia's wedding dress, but if we get started right away, I am sure we can do this."

"Ahh Beth, you are wonderful, thank you, thank you. There is one more thing...? I also need the bridesmaids' and flower girls' dresses as well."

I held my breath. This was a massive commission, and I only had a month to complete what would normally take a minimum of three months.

You can do this Beth.

Breathing out slowly I replied, "Ok, Ellen my dear, we are meeting on Thursday anyway, so let's discuss everything then. Is that ok?"

"Perfect Beth, thank you so much, see you on Thursday." It was lovely to hear her voice so excited, however, I could not believe all of this was happening so fast. That evening I sat with Holy Spirit as we talked about the day.

"I don't understand this Holy Spirit!"

"What don't you understand?" He questioned, not looking up from the information I was typing on the computer.

"Why would I get this order at this time?" I replied, getting a little agitated that He appeared to be more interested in what I was typing than what I was saying. "Why now? Why didn't I get this order when I had my studio? I needed this kind of money back then to pay the bills and when I had the facilities to make these dresses! Why is this happening now?" My throat tightened as I tried to fight back the tears.

Holy Spirit came and sat next to me and waited for me to calm down. He put his hands on my shoulder.

"Beth, Father loves you very much and He knows how

much the studio meant to you and how much it hurt you to give it up, but you are going to have to trust Him with this. Come let me show you."

I reached for my Bible and opened it. As I read about seasons, Holy Spirit and I went into the throne room of my heart. I walked over to Jesus and embraced Him.

"Beth, you must trust Father like Holy Spirit says," Jesus' voice was so comforting, "Please don't try to work out everything by yourself."

"I know, but when I think of my bridal studio I can't help being upset," I admitted.

"Don't forget what you read tonight. Seasons of your life change and you have to respond. You will see that a busy life and an effective life are very different. Let Holy Spirit guide you and teach you all you need to know."

I knelt beside Jesus and rested my head on His lap. He put His hands on my head and stroked my hair. He began to sing over me and as He sang, a sense of peace fell over me. I turned and found myself back in my room. I switched off the lights and settled down to sleep.

The next few weeks were hectic, as I worked hard to create the designs for Ellen and Sophia. I was working, without being able to have many consultations with them, which was not my usual practice. I threw myself into the challenge, and Holy Spirit constantly guided me so that I was able to get it all done in record time. Tracy was instrumental in me completing everything. She ordered the bridesmaids' dresses for me so that I could simply alter them to size. After much discussion, Ellen chose the flower girls' dresses from designs I had made at my studio. Everything was coming together perfectly, and I found that I was really enjoying the challenge.

Soon it was time for me to fly to Italy to take the dresses. They were tacked and prepped as best as I could, but I needed Sophia and Ellen to try them on before I could complete them. They had agreed to supply me with sewing machines when I arrived in Italy so that I could continue working.

The week before I was due to leave, Mia pregnant with her first child, was admitted into hospital. The doctor didn't give us much hope of her survival or that of the unborn child if she went through with the pregnancy. They suggested aborting the child to give Mia a chance of treatment. But that was not an option for her. I felt my trust and faith in Jesus being pulled and stretched to its limit as I wrestled with the news.

"Mom I'll be fine, Stephen is here with me, and you know Jesus is looking after me.

"But Mia."

"Seriously Mom, this is a huge opportunity for you. Go get it, and stop worrying. I'll see you when you get back."

Trying to persuade Mia was a pointless venture, so I talked it over with Holy Spirit and by faith trusted her into the hands of Jesus.

The plane ride was a mixture of excited anticipation and apprehension of what I was going to encounter in Italy. I looked out the cabin window at the lush vegetation down below and breathed in the warm Italian air. Travelling alone was a new experience for me, I had always had Raoul or the children to entertain me. But secretly, I was enjoying the peace and quiet to gather my thoughts. This was always what I wanted for my business - to travel, and now it was actually happening.

The cabin door opened and I stepped out onto the top of the plane steps into the sticky summer heat. I breathed steadily trying to be the grownup I was supposed to be, but fearing everyone in the airport could see that I was completely afraid. I had never done anything like this before - travel abroad to dress a bride and her family. I shook my head to still my thoughts. *No, Beth,* I thought to myself, *you are more than able to do this.* I was a designer, I was an entrepreneur. I lifted my head high and began to walk purposefully.

Dragging my suitcase behind me I arrived at the airport lounge and was greeted by waving hands, and huge smiles. Ellen and her family had all come out to greet me, even their dog was friendly as he rounded my legs, sniffing his approval.

"I'm so glad you're here, Beth." Ellen was now hugging me tightly, and the fear began to disappear.

"Ah Beth I can't wait to see my dress!" Sophie excitedly embraced me.

"Hi everyone," I said sheepishly, slightly overwhelmed by their kind welcome.

"Let's get you settled," Ellen declared, as she signaled to her husband, Matt, to take my bags.

They drove me to the hotel where I was to spend the

next few days. We pulled up outside a modern building, rows of glass windows scaling upwards. *Wow, Beth, you have truly arrived,* flitted into my mind. I was signed in and escorted to my suite.

The door opened into a long corridor, lined with wardrobes, and doors leading to different rooms. Ellen and Sophia chatted excitedly as I walked down the corridor into a huge lounge. Large bay windows, opened to reveal a long veranda and a stunning view overlooking the sea.

"Is this good for you?" Ellen asked walking around inspecting each room. "If it's not big enough I will find somewhere else for you in the morning," she continued before I had a chance to answer.

"Oh, no, this is wonderful!" I looked around in amazement.

I turned off the corridor into a large bedroom with a double bed which looked so inviting that I couldn't wait to curl up into it.

"Are you sure? I want you to be comfortable and happy while you are here with us," Sophia joined in, as she signaled to the porter where to put the bags.

"We are very grateful to you for coming at such short notice. I don't know how we would have sorted out this dilemma without you," Ellen said her eyes filling up with tears. "Please, let us know if there is anything else you need and we will have it brought to you. The machines and everything on the list you sent me will be here first thing in the morning," Ellen assured me.

"Thank you, this is so lovely," I smiled at her. If only

she knew how both privileged and honoured I felt at that moment. I had not expected anything so grand.

"Ok, I will leave you to get settled in and we will talk business tomorrow," she said as she dried her tears.

"Did you remember to bring an evening gown?" Sophie asked as they prepared to leave.

"Yes," I replied, "your Mom told me to, I didn't really know what to bring…" I started to explain but before I could finish, Sophie and Ellen were moving towards the door.

"That's great!" Sophie said clapping her hands in excitement.

"Thank you again Beth and we will see you in the morning," Ellen said as she ushered Sophie out the door. They both waved goodbye and left.

I was left to the silence of the hotel suite. A grin filled my face.

"Do you see this Holy Spirit!"

"I do, perfect for a Princess," He smiled.

"Uh I could get used to this." I spun round on the veranda, the sun shining down on my face.

I raced into the bedroom, leapt onto the bed and exhaled. My mind was racing with everything I had to do within the week - the alterations, the fittings, I had to be on top of things. They had done so much for me, far beyond what I had imagined.

"Sounds like you had a hand in this, Father," I smiled upwards giving thanks to Him. I rested my head on the fluffy pillow, excited to be experiencing such favour, such grace.

"Holy Spirit, what is grace?" I realised I had used the word but didn't actually know what it meant.

"Well, it is unmerited favour. Actually it's more than that, it's the ability to do more with God than you could ever do on your own. Imagine what else you could believe for, if you dared."

I eyed Holy Spirit suspiciously, "My father has always said that we shouldn't be money-minded or crave for things. He always taught us it is better to give." I lifted my head proudly, sure I knew best.

"Yes the love of money is a problem, but I'm talking about stretching out your faith and believing God for more. Everything He has is yours, He loves you. How can you give, if you don't have anything to bless others with?"

I sat pondering what Holy Spirit had said. I sure felt as though I was experiencing more than I could have, if I was doing things on my own. Look at my bridal studio, it was great, but nothing compared to this. I considered that maybe Holy Spirit had a point. There were so many women that I had wanted to help, but I never had the resources to really make a difference. *What if I did believe for more?* I closed my eyes, imagining what my life would be like if I didn't put any limits on myself, or on God. A smile crept across my face as thoughts and images came flashing through my mind, things that on my own would be impossible.

I finished the order within the week. Out of the corner of my eyes, I could see Holy Spirit watching smiling as I pressed and hung up the wedding dress, the bridesmaids' dresses and Ellen's dress, ready for collection. He didn't say much, but His presence made me feel at peace after my hectic week. I also knew that if anything was wrong with the dresses, He would have told me. So I rested and trusted that all was well.

I made a cup of tea and sat on the veranda, looking out at the sea as the waves gently splashed and rolled onto the sand in the distance. Holy Spirit came and sat next to me and we both sat watching the stars glistening in the sky.

"Isn't this lovely Holy Spirit," I breathed in the beautiful sight and smell of the sea.

"Yes it is beautiful."

"Sophia's wedding dress looks amazing now that it's finished. Thank you for helping me, I couldn't have done all that work without you," I said putting my empty cup on the little table in front of me.

"You are welcome," he turned to me and took my hand in his. "Remember when the disciples had fished all night and didn't catch anything?" He asked.

"Yes," I replied with a quizzical expression.

"Then Jesus turned up and told them to cast their nets on the other side."

"Umhmm."

"And they caught so much fish that they had to ask for help?"

"Yes! That's just how I feel right now," I continued looking directly at Him.

"Go on," He said slowly, one eyebrow arched, as he released my hand, giving me room to express my thoughts.

"Well, I felt like those disciples in that boat when I was at the studio. I tried everything I knew to keep the customers coming. I even 'toiled' all night to get orders finished and thought of creative ways to stay afloat, but I still had nothing to show for all my hard work except some thread and unused fabric, just like the disciples and their empty nets. Then you came and nudged me into accepting change and taking that job at the bridal shop and now I'm here doing what I do best, but what a new experience!" I said animatedly as I stretched out my arms.

"You've got it!" Holy Spirit laughed as we held hands and started to dance.

The next morning I was woken up to the sound of the alarm clock blaring from my phone. I reached over to the bedside table and slowly turned it off, struggling to focus on the screen. I did not want to wake up - it was the first sound sleep I had had all week. Then it hit me, it was wedding day! I jumped out of bed and quickly got myself ready. This was Sophia's big day and I wanted to make sure I had everything sorted to ensure she felt like the beauty she was.

Sophia and Ellen arrived early and in no time had arranged for the bridesmaids' dresses to be picked up. When everyone had left, I took Sophia's wedding dress out of the wardrobe and hung it on the doorframe. This was the first time she would see the finished product beaded and pressed. As I unveiled the dress, both Sophia and Ellen covered their mouths in amazement.

"It's beautiful!" they both gasped in unison. Sophia threw her arms around me and hugged me, as tears streamed down her face and onto my shoulders.

"It's more beautiful than I could have ever imagined. Words cannot express how happy you have made me today," she said as she tenderly admired the dress. Ellen sat down on the chair and just allowed her tears of joy to flow freely as she stared at the dress.

"Beth, where did you find time to do all that beading?" she asked breathing deep in an effort to catch her breath. "You couldn't have slept! You must be an angel sent from God," she continued.

Well that was a first! I had been called many things before, but never an angel! After half an hour of 'cooing' and 'ahhing' the plans of the day were revealed. Ellen and Sophia would take the wedding dress to the house and return to pick me up in an hour. I was to have my evening gown and everything I would need for the day ready to take with me when they returned. For the first time since arriving in Italy I felt anxious. Butterflies were fluttering around in my stomach refusing to let even hot water settle it.

"Holy Spirit, what is making me feel so uneasy?" I shook myself trying to steady my nerves.

"Maybe it's because you can't see what's ahead, but you just have to trust the process, just like Ellen trusted you with the most important dress and event of her daughter's life."

"You're right as usual Holy Spirit. This trust issue of mine isn't getting any easier is it?!" I exclaimed as I started packing my things.

"Just remember who your Father is and that you are a Princess. I will be right there with you," He assured me patting my hand.

"Thank you Holy Spirit." I hurried from room to room in an effort to get ready. I packed my things and was ready just as the door knocked. It wasn't Sophia or Ellen. It was Ethan, Ellen's son.

"Hi. Are you ready?" he asked casually.

"Yes I'm ready," I picked up the keys and headed for the door where he was waiting.

"We are going to my parent's house where the bridal party is getting ready."

"Okay." I tried to calm my nerves as we drove about a mile to the house. I kept repeating to myself, *I don't have fear, I have love and a strong mind.*

The house was bustling with activity when we arrived and I was ushered up an elegant long staircase, to one of the many rooms on the first floor. Sophia greeted me with a smile. She looked radiantly beautiful with her black hair pined up in curls, complimented with a tiara and her make-up freshly applied. We chatted as I dressed her and then I went to her mother's room to help Ellen get dressed. When they were ready, I was taken to where the bridesmaids were waiting and tied bows and zipped up dresses. I was then ushered to where the men were and fixed bowties and collars.

When all the men left for the church and I thought I was going to have a break, Ellen called me.

"Beth! Come up and get ready the cars will be here

soon," she said anxiously. I ran back up the stairs to where Ellen was standing.

"Get ready!?" I asked surprised.

"Yes, yes, the photographers are here already and you have to take pictures with us," she said directing me to her room and showing me where the bathroom was before disappearing down the stairs. The penny dropped. The gown wasn't merely for the after party as I had thought, but for me to take pictures with the family and be a part of the bridal party. I couldn't believe it! My heart started pounding in fear, my mouth became dry, as I hurried to get ready.

"Are you ready my dear?" Ellen called from downstairs.

"Yes I'm coming!" I looked in the mirror and took a deep breath.

Don't be afraid. Remember who your Father is. Hold your head up Princess.

"Thank you Holy Spirit." I whispered and made my descent. The photographers started taking pictures.

"Hold it just there," one said.

"Lovely," said another.

"Turn to the side a little."

"Great."

"Walk down."

"You look like a film star," said the video-man as he reached out to take my hand at the last step.

"Thank you," I replied as I was ushered into the sitting room where the family were having their pictures taken.

"Here she is!" Ellen exclaimed as she held my hands

and stood me with the family the cameras clicking away.

The cars arrived and I was about to sit on a chair to wait for the bridal party to leave, when Ellen held my hand pulling me in the direction of the front door.

"Come Beth. You will be travelling with me," she said as we hurried to the waiting car.

When we arrived at the church, lining up for the bridal procession, Ellen again held my hand and stood me right next to her at the very front of the procession and before I had time to think about what was happening, the organ started to play and the procession was ready to walk in. As we walked into the Cathedral, I realised that this was a wedding of opulence and a family of status. *No ordinary person would have the privilege of getting married in this place,* I thought to myself. What an honour bestowed on me by this wonderful family! My stomach turned somersaults, I took a deep breath and smiled trying to keep in step with Ellen. As we walked up the aisle, I remembered what Holy Spirit told me earlier. So I held my head up like a child of a King and walked up the aisle with dignity. Right the way through the whole day, I was treated like a guest of honour and given family status throughout my stay.

On the plane journey home, I reflected on the whole experience. Wow! I had not expected for my life to have included such a journey. I had slumped my head in fear on the way to Italy, afraid of what I would have encountered. But now my head was held high, I was truly the child of a King. If this was what happened when I trusted God, then I couldn't wait to see what other grand things He had in store for me. I began to 'stretch my neck out' and believe for more just as Holy Spirit had advised me to. What did I have to lose?

Chapter 14
Burden

I arrived home from Italy and went straight to Mia's house. She looked as well as could be expected but the pregnancy was taking its toll on her body, but not on her faith. She was confident that what God had promised her and Stephen would come to pass and she would not tolerate any fear around her.

I was back home, resting in front of the TV, tired from a long day, when my phone rang. It was Stephen.

"Is everything ok?" I said missing out all normal pleasantries.

"Umm, Mia says something doesn't feel right. She's called the hospital they want her to come in straight away. We're on our way to get you now."

"Right, fine, I'll be ready." I threw my phone down and leapt from the settee, pacing up and down the living room, I screamed.

"Jesus! Remember you promised I could trust you and I'm trusting you. Holy Spirit tell Him! Remind Him what He promised me! Send the angels to surround her now, PLEASE. I need you!"

She's in my hands and I've got her covered.

I was panting now, I daren't think of the worst case scenario. No, I couldn't go there. I heard Stephen's car horn, grabbed my coat and raced to the car.

The doctor gently advised that preparations should be made for the baby to be delivered that night. It was now around 2.30am and I had no strength to pace the floor, I was physically and mentally tired. The tiredness absorbed every feeling of emotion. This was not the normal new grandmother experience that I had hoped for. No, this was the anxiety of a mother waiting to hear if her daughter and granddaughter were to live.

"Don't worry Mom," Mia said casually looking up at me from the chair she was sitting on in the doctor's office. "If I die through this, I will just get to heaven before you and I will see you later."

I shook my head, I didn't want to hear that, and it didn't make me feel any better. I wanted to hold her, I wanted to take the whole experience away from her.

A nurse appeared to take Mia and Stephen through to the operating theatre.

"Are you ok?" Mia's mouth mimed, as they wheeled her away. I responded with a nod and she was gone.

Silence. They say silence is deafening, well this silence was unbearable. I sat staring at the blank white walls consciously listening, trying to hear something that would give me a clue as to what was happening. But it just echoed back its agonising stillness. I wanted to cry, but couldn't. The tears, then the sobs that would shake my tired body, the holding of my stomach to try to calm myself, I didn't have the strength for all that…no, no tears today. I tried to go into the throne room of my heart, to find a safe place, but I couldn't. I tried to remember Bible verses to ease the pain that wanted to burst into a scream, to stop the pressure that was crushing every organ in my body. But my mind remained locked. It was then I heard a whisper.

She is in my hands, I have her covered.

I whispered back as though not wanting to disturb the silence.

"Thank you Jesus."

The nurses came back and forth every now and then. As they walked past the open door, I would look up at them wide-eyed, hoping to hear something, anything, any news.

"Would you like a cup of tea, dear?" a nurse asked dutifully. But she had no news.

"Oh yes please," I sighed.

"Are you ok?" another asked, as she popped her head around the door.

"I'm fine thank you," I lied.

"It won't be long now."

"Oh great," I responded like a programmed robot.

The tea came, not just in a mug, but a teapot on a silver tray with sugar, milk, a cup and saucer, with a teaspoon carefully placed. I thanked the nurse, then thanked Father for the nurse that took the trouble to make me feel so special. I was sure she had been an angel, because I had not seen any NHS teapots before.

You are my Princess and I love you.

I smiled and sipped the hot tea that warmed my empty stomach reminding me that I hadn't eaten since breakfast and it was now 3am. My stomach rumbled to confirm my thoughts.

At last the nurse came with the long awaited announcement.

"It's a girl!" she beamed, "all went well. You can see her in a while just wait here and someone will come and get you." Then she was gone! They hadn't told me anything about Mia.

So I sat in the hospital room waiting, tired to the point of soreness, a volcano of emotions waiting to erupt. I was exhausted. The day's events started running through my head like a pack of hungry wolves, eating up any positive thoughts I had left. The quietness filled the room and echoed in my ears, I quickly covered them to block out the silence!

My peace I give to you. Don't let your
heart be anxious.

I whispered back, "thank you."

At last I was taken to see Mia. My body ached from the hours sitting and waiting, my mind racing as I walked down the corridor to her room. I watched her lying there so still, just the sound of the machines humming out a sound of hope and a nurse watching over her. I wanted to cry but not here not now, *please God not now.* I swallowed hard to fight back the tears. I wanted to hug her and tell her how much I loved her, but I couldn't, the machines and wires wouldn't let me. So I blew her a kiss and whispered, "I love you."

The emotional volcano that had been building inside me all day was now about to erupt. Everything inside me was screaming, *FATHER, PLEASE!*

> *She shall not die but live to declare my glory.*

Finally, Stephen appeared to take me to see the baby. As we entered the room the nurse smiled.

"She's doing really well," she said leading the way to where the baby slept. I looked, but couldn't see a baby, it just looked like a large glass bowl with wires and lights! Heavy-eyed I looked again.

> *I have not given you a spirit of fear*
> *but of power, love and a sound mind.*

"Thank you Lord."

And there she was a tiny little baby girl, beautiful all 3lbs 3ozs of her.

> *She shall not die but live to declare my glory.*
> *I make all things possible.*

Mia and Stephen named the baby Kara. Although tiny she was a fighter, strong and full of hope. Against all odds, she defied doctors' limitations and within three weeks both Mia and Kara were out of the hospital and back home.

After the birth of my granddaughter, Mia needed an

organ transplant. It wasn't possible for me to give her the organ she needed, so my son offered instead. This was very noble of him, and I was relieved to know that Mia had a chance of a normal life, but the cost was great. I felt like Abraham tying his son to the altar ready to sacrifice him. Only for me this was not one sacrifice, but two, as both my children would be on the operating table at the same time. I spoke to Jesus many times about Mia's illness, but He kept telling me to 'let go'. I rested on my bed contemplating why Jesus didn't just heal her and why did He keep telling me to let go? In my distress I went into the throne room to talk to Jesus, I needed intervention, not mere talking.

"Beth I know you are hurt and angry with the whole situation and believe me I feel your pain," He said reaching out to take my hands as I approached Him.

"Jesus I feel like I have let go like you asked, so how much more letting go must one mother do?!" I said thumping the air in my frustration and confusion, "It would solve the whole situation if you would just heal her, Jesus, why don't you just heal her?" My resolve broke as my voice trailed into silence. I covered my face with my hands and sobbed.

"Beth, your way isn't my way. I don't think like you. You must trust me with this. I have a perfect plan for Mia and Benji's life." He stood and held me close. I could hear His heartbeat, the rhythm drawing me into a sense of calm.

As I left the throne room, I found myself in bright daylight. I was walking down a road, in my arms was a load bigger and heavier than I was. I don't know who gave me the load or where it came from, but all I knew was I couldn't put it down and no one was around to help carry it. I couldn't quite see what the heavy load was at first glance, because my eyes were blurred from the brightness of the sun. I could feel the weight straining every muscle in my body, making me groan. I knew I had to put it down, but not just anywhere; it had to be somewhere safe, but I couldn't see where. I blinked so I could see a little clearer, trying hard to focus on the weight that was causing me so much pain. I could not believe it, there was my Benji lying limp and lifeless across my arms. I stumbled slightly trying to hold him closer. *What had happened to him? Why was he so lifeless?*

"Benji! Benj!" I shook him slightly, trying to wake him. "Wake up, come on Benj, please!" He made no movement and with every moment that passed, holding him was becoming more and more difficult. I was becoming frantic, *Where can I put him down? Someone please help!*

"Jesus where are you?" I whispered, my heart, aching.

If you seek me with all your heart you will find me.

This is not a good time for you to be elusive Jesus! I thought furiously as I looked around in hysterical panic. Panting for breath, I willed my heart to keep beating, as my arms struggled to hold on. I was stumbling now, my legs about to give up when there in the distance I saw Him. Strength came from deep inside, every step filled with a mother's determination, I heaved Benji to Jesus.

He was sitting on the steps of a large church building. He appeared unconcerned that I was carrying my heavy, fragile load. In fact His head was buried in a book reading! *Surely He heard me as I was approaching Him, after all, my steps were so loud and my breathing so heavy.* I wanted to shout like the disciples, when Jesus was asleep in the boat, undaunted by the storm beating up on the boat. *Can't you see that I am struggling here? How could you sit and read a book at a time like this!* But I didn't have the strength to shout, so between faint panting breaths I whispered, "Jesus". I didn't think He heard. My mouth was parched and I was completely drained, but He immediately looked up and caught my son, who was by now falling from my throbbing arms. I dropped my exhausted body on the step, next to Jesus in relief. My heart pounding like Conga drums, my head thumping in rhythm, tears fell from my eyes like a cooling waterfall.

"Jesus, please will you hold my son?" I asked wearily, "I need to go and see Father."

"Yes, no problem," He replied cradling my son in his arms. I took one last look at my son's lifeless body in the arms of Jesus. *He'll be alright,* I told myself, He was safe now, Jesus had him. I had to get to Father, I needed Him to fix this, He would know exactly what to do.

"Jesus, what's the password to get through security?" I asked my body feeling stronger with every passing moment.

"J.E.S.U.S"

As I looked up His eyes twinkled with compassion and I felt no condemnation, only love and the assurance that my son would be ok.

"Thank you," I replied and rushed off in the direction of the throne room to see Father, but the painful scene started repeating! This time I was carrying Mia. She looked cold and unconscious in my arms, no different from the agonising reality a few months before. Father promised me back then that my daughter would not die, but live to proclaim His glory and He kept that promise. *So why is she so lifeless? What has gone wrong?* My heart broke. The pain of disappointment tore through every inch of my body. Doubt began to race through my head like a sprinter to the finish line, with faith trying hard to outrun him. The situation was fraught with impossibilities. *I have to get her to Jesus. He will keep her safe while I go and talk to Father.* So with every ounce of strength I could find in me, I reached to where Jesus was sitting. He was still holding my precious son.

"Jesus, could you hold Mia as well please? I really need to go and see Father." Before I could finish the sentence His arms were outstretched, relieving my aching body of its burden.

"Thank you," I said. I felt stronger as He placed His hands around my shoulder. There was something about being with Him that seemed to make things come alive. Reaching into His pocket, He pulled out a tissue and dried my tears.

"Beth, Mia and Benji are going to be alright," He reassured me. "I have them covered."

"Thank you," I replied, as I ran off in the direction of the throne room.

Suddenly I heard a haunting noise, loud and eerie. Piercing laughter then filled the air, it was gone as quickly as it came. The atmosphere seemed to simply dissolve it. I spun around trying to see what had made the awful sound and there was he was, running at speed, heading straight towards me. I ducked out of his way as he steamed past me screeching with laughter.

"You'll never get to God before me, I know all the shortcuts. I've been using this route long before you were even born. By the time you get there I would have pleaded my case and left," he teased, his voice trailing off into the distance as he got further away from me. My heart sank - he was right, whoever he was, he seemed to know the way much better than I did. But deep inside me there was a feeling of urgency. I had to get to Father and it didn't matter even if he managed to get there first. I knew Father would have time for me, He always did. So I kept on running, trying hard to avoid the traps and diversions that he had put in the way. It was then I noticed an angel running alongside me, guiding my every step and reaching out to catch me every time I tripped up. Holy Spirit was also running along on the other side.

"Don't worry about the things Satan says, just concentrate on the things that Jesus said." So that was Satan. *Ok maybe Jenice was right. He really didn't like me at all!* I ran on trying hard to remember what Jesus told me a few days before.

I will never leave you, I will always be with you.

I kept on running knowing that I was not alone. At last I arrived at the throne room. I couldn't remember the last time I had run like that. Holy Spirit and the angel helped me up the steps. This was unfamiliar, not at all like last time I had come when I met Father. *Why was there a door to the Royal Throne Room? It didn't have a door before!* I punched in the password J.E.S.U.S and pushed the door open. Pushing the questions to the back of my mind I ran up the corridor. *Where did this corridor come from?* This was really weird! I ran past the angels to where Father was seated. This wasn't the Royal Throne Room, this was a court room!

Satan was already there, making his petition and putting it over very eloquently. His words were like a dagger stabbing my heart, as he blurted out his accusations against my children and me. Everything we had ever done, things I had completely buried, sins I had overlooked, he viciously spat them out before Father. I took my hands to my head and closed my eyes. This couldn't be happening, I had wanted to ask Father's help for my children. And now Satan, had His full attention. *Why would He ever want to listen to me, after He has heard all the depravities of my life?* Longingly, I looked up to the balcony where my children were lying in the arms of two angels, Goodness and Mercy. *But where is Jesus? He promised to look after them!* My eyes quickly scanned the room, *Where is He?* My focus was diverted back to Satan's dramatic display as I heard him yell,

"On these legal grounds they should die!"

Before I could respond, Mercy stood in front of my children and shouted, "NO!" Drama was unfolding right before my eyes as the angels of death and life stood face to face. "NO! You powers of darkness, I will never let them go!" Satan started a loud protest. Father called for order giving me a chance to defend myself and plead my children's case. I fell on my knees and bowed before Father. I couldn't look at Him because I knew everything Satan had said was true. It was then I remembered something Holy Spirit said to me as we were running along earlier,

Don't worry about the things Satan says, just think about the things that Jesus said.

So I slowly raised my head from its bowed position and looked at Father, remembering all the loving words Jesus had said. I removed my rucksack of condemnation from off my back and placed it on the floor as our eyes met.

"Father, I know that Satan had the right to ask for the death penalty, before you adopted me as your daughter. But I come to you on the legal grounds of your written Word, and all the promises you gave me through your Son Jesus. You promised that if I own up to the things I do wrong, you will keep your promise to immediately forgive me. I confess I have messed up, but I also confess Jesus is my Lord and King." I stood up slowly from my knees and continued. "You also said that I can come boldly to your throne of grace. So I stand before you today and I counter-petition Satan's claim on my life and the lives of my children."

Well, Satan was having none of it, he glared at me, and continued to argue against me, angry that I dared to think I could get away with my sin.

"She should be punished!" he declared, "nothing short of a death sentence will do."

Then suddenly as if everything went in slow motion, Father lifted His hands and clapped them together. The sound ricocheted like thunder across the room, creating instantaneous hush. As I looked to my right Jesus was standing next to me, all eyes were on Him. His arms slowly stretched open. The sleeves on His robe gently fell back to expose His hands. And there they were the marks from the nails that pierced His hands when He died on the cross, a permanent reminder that He now lives so that I too may live. Father looked at Jesus, turned and looked at me. He then turned and looked up at my children sitting with the angels Goodness and Mercy.

"Their sin was fully punished on the cross," He announced, "there is no more punishment to be carried out. They shall not die but live to declare my glory. Case dismissed!"

I woke up surrounded by an awesome presence. Holy Spirit appeared like a bright powerful light.

"Beth, you no longer have to worry about your children, but it is up to you to make the choice to let go and allow Father's perfect plan to be worked out in them."

"I hear you Holy Spirit." I breathed deeply with the reassurance that Jesus had them in His hands and they were covered just as He promised. This humbled me as I went into the throne room of my heart to worship. For the first time I wasn't dancing by myself. Holy Spirit came, held me and led me in a dance of worship. At the end of the dance I sat at Jesus' feet.

"Beth, Father loves you and waits for you to come and talk with Him. Satan will try every trick in the book to stop you from getting there, but I have provided everything you need to help you. You just have to come by faith, because without it you cannot please Him."

"Thank you Jesus. I will try and remember." I left the throne room feeling free and surprised at how different my worship was when I allowed Holy Spirit to lead.

Chapter 15

Gifts

Worrying came easy to me - it was a natural part of me. Mothers who cared for their children worried about them, didn't they? I had let go of carrying my children, but I often found myself worrying about the little things. Holy Spirit was asking me to not to worry, and not to fret about anything. It felt odd. When my children were sick, I was told not to worry. When my car broke down, no fretting. When I was out of work, trust me. And today it felt like giants of fear, and worry, were my companions.

I stood in front of the group for the first time - my mouth dry, my palms sweaty. I had something to say, it was there on my cue cards. But I couldn't see them, the words had muddled into a fuzzy blur. *Breathe, Beth, breathe,* I told myself. I looked up to a sea of faces, waiting expectantly for me to start.

I had practised this. Susan my new mentor and friend,

had taught me all I needed to know to cope with this moment.

"Take a deep breath, Beth, if you get nervous, then simply begin. You will find that the words will just start to flow."

Susan had a wisdom that made it easy to listen to what she taught. Although small in stature she had a manner that made you instantly relax around her. She had a heart for people that showed through her kind actions and words of encouragement. No question was too ridiculous and, if there was something she was unsure of, she would say, "I'll pray and look into that and come back to you". Sure enough she would call or visit with an answer. There was never any condemnation when she spoke, which made me comfortable enough to confide in her.

"I meet Jesus in a garden!" I blurted out, at one of her visits to my home.

"Umm hmm." No change in her voice, or reaction on her face.

"And He talks to me," I continued. She nodded in agreement, "I invited Him into a throne room...which is in my...heart."

That's it she's going to think I am crazy!

"Ahhh that's awesome!" she bounced on the settee in excitement, "go on tell me more!"

"Well umm, I've also met Father, in His throne room. That was an amazing experience! He wasn't anything like I'd expected."

I was on a roll now. She had not declared me insane, and had actually become more and more excited the more

I spoke. I told her about Holy Spirit and how I spoke to Him regularly during the day; how I could hear Him speak; and that sometimes I could feel how He felt about something, like a nudging inside of me.

"That's what I like to hear. A true unique experience with God. That's your relationship with Him, now that's what I call freedom!"

"Really! You don't think that's a little…strange."

"Ah Beth, it's so exciting when you know God for yourself, don't ever doubt your spiritual walk with Him."

"Spiritual walk?"

"Well yes, you learn the most about God when you walk in spirit and in truth. Holy Spirit is the best guide for that."

"Spiritual, sounds a bit weird like gory vampires and spooky ghosts to me," we both laughed.

She touched my arm, "This is your body, but there is so much more to you that you cannot see. You are actually a spirit that has a soul and lives in a body."

I narrowed my eyes, "I am a spirit. That seems a little farfetched Susan."

"Really," she smiled, "then explain how you can see into the spirit world, and it be so real to you?"

I stopped. I hadn't thought about that. The garden, the throne room, all felt tangible to me, more real than the very settee we sat on.

"You see Beth, the unseen world is just as real as the seen. Your faith allows you to access all of it. Not just the physical, bodily part of you but the spiritual unseen too. It's amazing if you consider the possibilities when you believe in Jesus." She was so animated, enthusiastically explaining who I really was. "I've got some friends I would love you to meet," she smiled.

Susan invited me to a Bible school called Academy for Life, which was held during the week and to the fellowship meeting on a Sunday morning. This was different from church as I knew it. It was unceremonious, interactive and fun. I was inspired and motivated by the way Susan taught, the way she captured everyone's attention, from the youngest to the oldest and in my heart I wanted to teach like that. Often during the service, Susan would allow people to share. Some came forward with images and visions that they had seen in the spirit. Others shared their dreams, a picture or a word that God had given them. It was here that I realised that the heavenly language I often worshipped in, could be interpreted, if God gave someone a translation. Spiritual experiences were commonplace, and I came to accept that my walk with Jesus was a normal part of my Christian life.

I sat in the meeting one Sunday morning listening attentively to Susan as she spoke about David and Goliath and compared them to the things that become giants in our lives. On my way home, as I walked in the warm glow of the sun, I reflected on what she had said.

"Oh Holy Spirit, there are so many giants in my life!" I said as I strolled along. I loved the opportunity to learn new things at the meetings, but not the challenge it provoked within me to change.

"Giants?" He stroked His chin as if in deep thought.

"Yes, the giant of 'failure' and 'fear' shouts at me every time I think about doing something different!" I said getting a little uptight, "just like that giant Goliath, shouting at the army of Israel."

"Well what are you going to do about it?" He questioned.

"I'll have to deal with it I suppose," I frowned at the thought. "The thing is I don't know where to start."

"Start from where you are Beth. Use what's in your hand."

"You mean pick up stones and sling it at them, like David did?" I laughed.

"Well that would be a start!" He said chuckling. "But seriously Beth, if you let the giant of fear and failure control you, you'll never discover the gifts Father has given you." His tone was sincere.

"I know Holy Spirit, I feel like I'm not using my gift as a designer anymore, but what else is there?" I sighed as my shoulders drooped.

"Beth, let me tell you a story," He said light-heartedly. "There was an employer who planned to take a holiday, but before he left he called three of the workers and gave them each an envelope marked 'A Special Gift'. They all opened their envelopes with excitement. In each envelope were practical ideas of how to make extra money."

"I could do with one of those," I said perking up, "sorry, carry on."

"The first employee was given just one practical idea with easy instructions, but he feared someone might steal his idea, or that he would fail at it and everyone would laugh at him, so he put it back in the envelope and hid it in a safe place. The other two employees used their 'special gifts' to their advantage. One gained double his monthly income and the other five times his monthly income, both adding to their career portfolio. When the boss returned from holiday, he called the three employees and asked them how they got on with the gifts he had given to them. He was impressed with the two employees who had used their gifts well and promoted them to even higher positions, but the employee that didn't use his gift was sacked and his gift taken away."

"Why did the employer take the gift away from the man that didn't use it? Why didn't he just encourage him to use it?" I asked irritated.

"The employee had the same opportunity to use it as the ones with two and three gifts, but he chose not to."

"Umm, so basically you are saying that I am not using a gift that Father has given me. Am I going to have to work this out, or are you going to tell me which gift I'm not using?"

Holy Spirit stayed silent. I rolled my eyes, *More work for me to do then.*

"Can you at least give me a hint?"

Susan invited me to attend one of the courses at her Bible school, called 'Bringing out the teacher in you'. Qualifying as a teacher was something I had always wanted to do, but going to a college to accomplish that dream was out of the question. I was never confident in a formal learning environment having spent much of my childhood either being too sick to attend school, or simply avoiding it. However, this course was informal and it made teaching seem like a skill I could achieve.

That was until that day, the day the giant of fear gripped me. I was standing in front of a group of people from the fellowship meeting. My assignment was to teach them on a subject I had prepared. I nervously introduced myself, and then looked back down to my cue cards, still a blur. I smiled at the audience and then as if I had been doing it my whole life, I began. Susan was right. Once I got started it really wasn't that bad.

I worked my way through the course, conquering different levels of the qualification. Each time the giant of fear and failure raised its ugly head, I would throw another stone of faith at it. By the time I'd finished the course, I was confident and ready to move on to formal learning.

My first formal job in teaching was outside the comforts of Academy for Life - at a training company. My role was to teach clients who needed skills to return to work. It was new and exciting at first, but I had to work hard to meet deadlines and reach targets. I had many years' practice in meeting deadlines whilst in previous employment and also in the confines of my own business, but this was different. The pressure was intense; the competitiveness between the staff members to gain management approval and make as much money as possible, was beyond my comprehension. Every waking hour was spent doing work related tasks, trying to keep up with the competition and the extra studies I had to do in order to have a formal teaching qualification. And there was more. I had to gain a qualification in every subject I was expected to teach. As one course finished, I was expected to move on to a higher level. There was also the stress of maintaining high standards of teaching practice and performance which was formally assessed every six weeks.

In my busy week, I tried to talk to Holy Spirit on the way to work and talk to Him again on the way home. Every night I would fall into bed physically and mentally exhausted. I didn't even have time to go into the throne room of my heart to talk with Jesus. In fact, I couldn't hear or see Jesus or Holy Spirit. I just took it for granted they would always be there. But I missed talking to Holy Spirit in the day, asking His opinion on the things I was doing or was about to say, allowing Him to show me and instruct me when I didn't know how to do a particular thing. My head and my heart began to physically ache and I caved in under the pressure. I needed rest, but most of all I wanted peace from the storms of work related targets and expectations.

I sat by the lounge window looking out into the garden. I wasn't focusing on anything in particular; I just needed to still my mind from the 'rush' of thinking that trundled through my head.

Closing my eyes, I went to the throne room of my heart to meet with Jesus. I was taken by surprise as I walked in. It looked like I was in a different place. There was so much noise I couldn't hear myself think. A party was going on and it didn't look like Jesus had planned it! Pity was the DJ, skilfully mixing the music that was blaring from two large speakers on the stage where Holy Spirit and I usually danced. No one appeared to notice that I had entered the room except Sorrow who handed me a glass of tears, which he poured from a black bottle. The room was packed with people I recognised, but wouldn't regard as friends. They all appeared to be having a good time laughing, drinking and dancing. I pushed past Worry who was sitting on a rocking chair talking to Stress and almost knocked the glass out of Guilt's hand as he danced wearily with Fatigue. I looked around the room and saw Depression leaning on the wall drinking by himself. Not too far from him was Discouragement swaying to the music with her eyes closed. I squeezed past Anxiety and Fear who were sitting by the throne. I overheard from Insignificance that it was Fear that had planned the party. *But where is Jesus?* My heart was feeling heavy as I ducked past Pain who was swinging his hands all over the place and stepped over Disappointment, who was sitting on the floor talking with Gossip. Holding my glass of tears, I walked past Condemnation sitting in a wheelchair and opened the door to the garden. I took a long deep breath relieved to be out of the stifling heat and there He was sitting on the doorstep.

"Jesus! What are you doing out here all by yourself?"

"I couldn't stay in there Beth," He answered softly as He turned and looked at me. His voice broke with sadness as He spoke. "The room got a little too crowded

221

and noisy for me." I sat on the step next to Him.

"I'm so sorry Jesus. I missed you so much." My cup of tears suddenly began to overflow onto my fingers, expressing exactly how I felt inside.

"Beth I love you," Jesus responded, His eyes dark with sadness as He watched me sip from my cup of tears.

"My life has been so chaotic and difficult without you. I didn't mean for this to happen, everything just spiraled out of control. Please forgive me." I knelt before Him, my heart feeling heavy.

"You are already forgiven," He said calmly. "You just have to accept my forgiveness," He reached out.

"Thank you Jesus," I took His hand. "Would you come and take your place on the throne of my heart?" I asked, my voice quivering as I tried to suppress the sobs.

"Of course I will my beloved."

We walked to the door and He stretched out His hand. I handed Him my cup of tears and in exchange He gave me a beautiful crystal glass, filled with joy. No words can explain the sheer exhilaration I felt as I sipped at this delightful nectar. I opened the door and invited Jesus into the throne room. Fear jumped up off the throne. There was an instant hush as Jesus walked over and took His place. His presence shone through the dimly lit room exposing everyone that was hidden by the darkness. Then there was chaos! Worry grabbed her rocking chair and ran through the door pushing Stress in front of her. Following suit Guilt began to bolt shouting to Pain to hurry if he wanted a lift because Gossip was driving. At the same time Sorrow grabbed a bottle of tears and shouted to

Pain, "Wait for me, I coming too!" Disappointment, Depression, Anxiety and Fatigue all got to the door at the same time and started pushing each other in an attempt to escape quickly. Condemnation shouted at them to move out of the way as he wheeled past them, followed by Discouragement and Pity who grabbed the last bottle of tears and left. Insignificance quietly crept out whispering goodbye to Fear, who was the last to leave. He gave me a warning gesture as he walked out the door.

At last Jesus and I were alone and together we cleaned up the mess left behind from my uninvited guests. Never once during our conversation did Jesus condemn me, but He repeatedly told me how much He loved me. When we finished the 'clean up', soothing, calm and soft music filled the room. Jesus took His place on the throne of my heart, and I danced in worship. Holy Spirit came and gracefully danced with me and ordered my steps, our feet moving in rhythm to the melodious music that filled the room.

Chapter 16
Bride

I felt clean, like pure water had cleansed my heart and I was free from all the negative feelings that had filled me. Jesus led me outside through the garden, down a smooth path and up a steep hill.

"Where are we going?" I asked, I had not been this way before.

"You'll see."

He was smiling now, like He had the best kept secret. I smiled back. It was wonderful to be walking together again. It made everything, easier. I had seen the effects of fear, how it had dominated and what it had done to my heart, how it had left Jesus outside. I was not about to go back there in a hurry. Instead I was learning to breathe, and rest in Jesus, He had everything in His hands. I smiled as I thought about how quickly worry and its friends simply fled, when Jesus took His place on the throne. I didn't just have the best friend I could ever ask for, but Jesus had power as well. He didn't even need to speak, just His presence made those emotions flee. What reason did I have to not trust Him? He was perfect.

We had stepped into a lush, green rainforest. The sun's rays beamed through the towering trees like needles of light. The humid air, the aroma of flowers and strange plants, made me feel a little giddy. As I walked slowly down the thin winding path covered in green moss, moist with humidity, I listened to the different sounds of the birds and insects. I cupped the unusual flowers in my hands, inhaling their beautiful fragrance. It was only then that I realised I was alone, Jesus and Holy Spirit had gone ahead without me. I wasn't afraid, the sounds of the rainforest were calming and peaceful as I strolled along. The winding path came to an end at a river, which sparkled brightly in the sun. I shaded my eyes from the brilliance of its reflection and followed the sound of splashing water and laughter. To my surprise, I saw Jesus and Holy Spirit dancing on the water. I sat by the water's edge watching them.

"Come on in!" Jesus beckoned.

"No thank you," I responded, "I'm not good in water, never mind on it!" I said laughing at their funny dance.

"Come on, you'll enjoy it," Jesus said stretching out His hands, "trust me."

"Umm, it does look fun, but You'll have to save me if I start to sink," I responded reluctantly as I rose to my feet. I took off my shoes and timidly dipped my toes in the shallow water and looked at Jesus.

"You realise my feet are going in the water, not on it," I said, doubtful that this was going to work.

"Keep walking. Don't look down, keep your eyes on me," He coaxed with His arms outstretched. I slowly lifted my head and looked at Jesus and to my surprise, I was stepping daintily on water.

"Ah ha, brilliant! I'm walking on water!" I laughed out, "Simon Peter eat your heart out!" Jesus started laughing too.

I reached to where Jesus and Holy Spirit were standing. They linked their arms in mine and began to dance. I moved along with them, enjoying the freedom of being on top of the water for a change, instead of panicking underneath it. Without warning, Jesus released my arm and Holy Spirit took me under the water.

I'm drowning! Help Holy Spirit, help! I thrashed about in fear, kicking and waving my hands around in an effort to stay alive. I tried to pull myself upwards towards the sea's surface, but Holy Spirit kept hold of me.

"Breathe," He said holding me around my waist.

Clearly I'm the only one who understands that I can't breathe under water. I wanted to shout at Him, I wanted to scream, that I wasn't a mermaid. I looked directly into His eyes, my face contorted from holding my breath for so long. I shook my head to tell Him that I couldn't breathe.

"Beth, breathe, it's ok, trust me."

I was going to die, Holy Spirit was obviously going to see to that. He turned my head back to His, and as I looked into His peaceful eyes again, a calm came over me and I stopped kicking and waving my arms about.

I took a small breath, certain the water would go straight into my lungs. But it didn't I was breathing. *How could I be breathing?!* I took another breath, and this time opened my mouth and blew out.

"Haha! Did you see that? I can breathe under water!" I cupped my mouth in shock. Clearly I could not only breathe under water, but also talk! Now this was truly fantastic.

"Oh my goodness, Holy Spirit, why didn't you tell me I could talk under water? So, can I also swim? I've never been able to do that before."

Holy Spirit smiled and took my hand. I was twirling and swimming like I had been living in water my entire life. I had conquered another fear, the fear of water. In my mind I threw another stone at the giant of fear and failure. Nothing was impossible to me when Holy Spirit and Jesus were around. I felt invincible. I lay on my back and kicked my legs, the water allowing me to glide through it.

"Come on now Beth," Holy Spirit signaled to the surface. I shook my head like a naughty child.

"No chance this is unbelievable, I like it here. I don't want to leave."

Holy Spirit simply smiled, and then slowly guided me to the surface. I found myself in my room talking in a heavenly language. I may have felt clean before, but now I felt truly cleansed, washed with water. Jesus and Holy Spirit had water I did not understand; I could walk on it and talk whilst in it. That was spiritual water I had never experienced before. A hunger grew within me, I wanted to experience all that God had for me.

"I am living the impossible," I shrieked, throwing myself backwards and worshipping God out loud.

After work the next day, I raced up to my room and went straight into the throne room of my heart. Yesterday had filled me with an excitement and an anticipation of what Jesus had in store for me next.

"Maybe I could fly this time," I giggled pushing the door to the throne room. Holy Spirit and Jesus were already there. They were both sitting at a table in deep conversation and didn't even look up when I entered the room. I saw their hands going up and down with a needle and thread. It looked like they were mending something. Not wanting to interrupt I tiptoed over to see what had made them both so engrossed. They were sewing jewels onto the most beautiful dress I had ever seen. I was sure I had seen this fabric before, but it looked different now. *Could this be the dress I am to wear on my special day?* I questioned in my mind. I stood riveted to the spot as Holy Spirit picked up a sparkling crystal and sewed it onto the sleeve. At the same time, Jesus picked up a diamond and secured it to the neckline. Curiously I moved in a little closer and noticed that these were no ordinary jewels! These were gems of faithfulness, forgiveness, love, trust and pearls of kindness. I held my breath in amazement and slowly retreated to my room. I threw myself onto my bed speechless. *That is some dress, but how can I wear it?* Just last week I was struggling, I had been consumed with fear and failure. No, this dress couldn't be for me!

That night I tossed and turned as the throne room

scene replayed in my mind. All the things I had done wrong that day flashed through my head like lightning on a stormy night. I tried to repeat all the things Holy Spirit had told me about who I had become and that Father saw me differently because I was now His daughter, but the lightning lit up my mind and smudged out the words and I couldn't see! So I ran into the throne room of my heart with frantic speed.

"Jesus, I need to go and speak with Father," I declared earnestly, as I ran through the throne room of my heart into the garden.

"Slow down!" Jesus said as He quickly rose from His seat and followed after me.

"I need to speak with Father," I repeated as He caught my hand in an attempt to slow me down.

"I heard you," He said gently, I began to slow down a little.

"I saw the dress Holy Spirit designed for me," I panted, trying to catch my breath.

"Umm, you did." He responded knowingly.

"Yes I did and I can't wear it!" I said defiantly, my voice shaking with the pace of my steps.

"Really, but why not?" He held my hand firmly which caused me to stop suddenly.

"I don't feel good enough and anyway I have put on loads of weight since He last measured me and it won't fit." I looked down at my feet. I couldn't look at Him, because deep in my heart I knew I wasn't making sense, but the words were out now and I couldn't take them back. "In fact the truth is, I just don't deserve it!"

"Beth, my beautiful rose," He said gently as He took both my hands, "my grace is all you need."

As He held me soft music filled the garden. He moved me around the garden to the music as it carried us into a waltz. I looked into His eyes as we danced, the aroma from the flowers reminding me of His unconditional love for me. I rested my head on His chest as He began to sing over me.

"Do not worry my love, wait patiently and I will show you great and amazing things that you could never imagine," He sang sweetly.

Suddenly I stopped dancing.

"You may feel that way Jesus, but what will Father think? He knows exactly who I am. He may not want me anymore."

"You have nothing to fear. You are the apple of my Father's eyes," He reminded me.

Slowly, we made our way to the Royal Throne Room entrance where Father was. I stopped at the doorway, deep in thought, considering exactly what I was going to say. That's when I realised.

"Oh no!" I gasped, holding out my night dress.

"What's the matter?" Jesus asked concerned.

"I didn't change my clothes!" I said in despair.

"Don't worry about it. Father won't even notice," His smile was reassuring. There was no going back now, I would have to approach exactly as I was, night clothes and all. I bowed my head and slowly took my first step towards Father. The Royal Throne Room was filled with angels, all worshipping God, creating a sweet aroma of praise. I blinked a few times to adjust my eyes to the brightness of the light that filled the room. It was electrifying, the praise of the angels was charging the atmosphere. I had stepped onto a blood red velvet carpet that lined the aisle all the way to the throne. It was so regal, I felt unworthy to step onto it in my slippers. I composed myself, lifted my head and consciously placed one foot in front of the other, my eyes focused on the throne.

I turned back to check Jesus was there with me, I didn't want to draw near to Father alone. He nodded and signalled to carry on. Suddenly my feet felt strange. I wiggled my toes, but could no longer feel the fluffy slippers I had been wearing. I stopped abruptly and looked down. There I stood in the most beautiful golden shoes, adorned with jewels. I looked away and looked down again to check I wasn't seeing things, but yes, I had somehow been dressed in shoes as I was walking. *Ok, wow, amazing!*

Intrigued to see what would happen if I kept on walking, I slowly proceeded towards Father. I smoothed my hands down my sides in an attempt to steady myself, and felt a silky luxurious fabric against my skin. I looked down, it was the lining of a dress, and at the bottom, layers of net bounced as I stepped. *It's an underskirt,* I laughed to myself, *I'm being clothed in the dress!* I was becoming excited now, I felt elegant already, and I didn't have the full dress on.

I turned again to look at Jesus, to find He was right next to me.

"This is awesome," I whispered.

"Wait till you see it completed, you are being robed," He answered.

Robed! Well this sure didn't look like a robe, I felt beautiful. I lifted my head high, and felt lace fabric against my skin that was trimmed with gold glistening thread. As I lifted my arm to examine its splendour, I then felt a light fabric encircle me and looked down to see that the lace had extended and was lying perfectly against my body, kicked out over the net. It was encrusted with glass crystals, diamonds, rubies and pearls. I spun around allowing the long flowing dress to sparkle as the light bounced off the jewels.

"Wow," escaped my lips. I didn't feel unworthy, I felt stunning, I felt like a Princess.

By the time I stood before Father, I was perfectly dressed. I bowed in reverence as He took a golden crown from the small table next to the throne and placed it on my head. Jesus reached out and took my right hand and slipped a golden ring of the highest honour on my finger. He then stretched out His hands and said,

"Come closer my Princess," and as my hands touched His, I realised my childhood dreams had finally come true. I was at this moment, a Princess of the Highest Royal Kingdom.

"Welcome Beth," I looked up into Father's eyes, and breathed a sigh of relief. His eyes of pure kindness beamed back at me and I was overwhelmed by His love for me. All my fears and insecurities about this moment, vanished. I was accepted, and a boldness filled me.

"This is amazing, thank You," I stood up, radiating the pure love that He had filled me with.

"Beth, you are my Daughter. Only the best is good enough for a child of the King. You are now robed in righteousness. Do you understand what that means?"

"Righteousness is a big word Father, and to be honest I have never felt that I could ever be righteous. That's what I came here to tell you."

"Well it means, you are clothed in Jesus' righteousness; it means that you are able to stand before me accepted. You can now freely become the person you were created to be, and do what I think is right."

"But I don't always get it right Father, and I don't want to leave here dressed in this beautiful righteousness and fail you."

"That's where Jesus comes in. Your righteousness will never match up to His. That's why it's a gift."

"So every time I come before You, in my own dress, You will actually see me perfectly dressed in Jesus' righteousness. I don't have to do anything?"

"Exactly, just have faith. Let Holy Spirit teach you and you will become more like Jesus day by day."

"Wow, You are so amazing God." I looked around at Jesus next to me, Holy Spirit smiling within me, and Father so tenderly accepting, and I realised I had it made. I may not be perfect, and I may be undergoing a process of change every day, but I was getting there. Here in the Royal Throne Room was my defining moment. I had overcome my past, I was working on my present, and by His grace I was going to dominate my future.

Acknowledgements

I couldn't have done this book without these special people on my team. The experience has been like giving birth and having the best midwives to help me through to a safe delivery. And what an extraordinary journey it has been!

Firstly, thank you Father, my Elohim Yahweh, Jesus, my Y'shua, for loving me even when I didn't deserve your love. It is because of You I have come this far and have lived to tell the story.

This journey started with you Sheila. "Sharon when are you starting the book?!" Thank you for the constant reminder and the encouragement to talk about what was my secret relationship with Jesus, Holy Spirit and Father. You made me feel 'normal.'

They call you Enid Weir, but I call you 'Mom'. You are so special to me. You have been my inspiration. Words cannot express my love and gratitude to you. You are a blessing, gift wrapped and sent straight from Father God to me, for such a time as this. Thank you for the 'cook food' when I had to write and had no time to cook - the only thing is now I have to exercise to get all this weight off! Thank you.

Tramaine, my beautiful gifted daughter, your editing and design skills. Wow!!! You have shown me what can be done when we take the inner limits off ourselves and the limits off God. Thank you for your self-sacrifice, your time and most of all your love and patience. You are my heartbeat. My special gift sent from heaven. Jerome, thank you for giving Tramaine time and space to help me through this process. Thank you Tiara for giving up your 'Mommy time,' so that she could help me with this book. I love you guys!

To my very special friend Novlett. Thank you for your words of encouragement and for sharing your unique gift of teaching with me - grammar was never my strong point! I'm sure you used a magnifying glass to find and correct every incorrect word. Thank you for your meticulous editing. Thank you for your time and selfless sacrifice. I love you my sister!

Thank you to my wonderful son Juvonne, for all your love and encouragement. I took a risk in writing this book and I learnt that from you, the original risk taker. When I look at you I see so much of myself, we think outside of the box that's why you have always understood me. Thank you for your acceptance I'm excited to see what God is going to do in your life.

A Message to Readers

Throne room of my heart is based on a true story, as I journey to discover that religion and relationship are very different. My heart has always longed to find Jesus in a very practical and authentic way. I am privileged that Jesus has always revealed Himself to me using my creative gift.

I have spent many years keeping my relationship with Jesus private as if I told anyone I went into the Throne Room of my Heart to meet with Jesus, I often received strange looks and a sympathetic sigh. Even Christians struggled to understand that Jesus is a real person that can give you a relationship with Him that is perfect for you.

I urge you to let Jesus into the Throne Room of Your Heart and pursue a real relationship with Him.

Sharon Corbett

Made in the USA
Charleston, SC
22 December 2015